Literary Biography

Reading Lists

Purple Rose Ink Publications

ISBN-13: 978-1530969401
ISBN-10: 1530969409

Reading: Lists and Stats

I knew that I read more than the average person, but by how much I wondered. Out of curiosity I checked how much the average American reads. One out of four people don't even pick up a book over the course of a year, which is just crazy to me. This means around 25% of people don't read regularly or read at all! One survey listed that the average amount of books read were between 4 and 7. Women read about 9 books a year while Men only read about 5 books a year. College Graduates read between 2 and 10 books a year on average. College Graduates also prefer nonfiction to fiction. My research also found that political leanings also factored in. Conservatives account for about 34% of NON-READERS. And Liberals accounted for about 22% of NON-READERS.

The National Education Association (NEA) reported that the number of adults who say they've opened a single book of fiction in the past year has dropped 14% in the last 10 years. This represents a general collapse in literacy throughout the beginning of the twenty-first century. They speculated that as many as 50% of adult Americans may simply be unprepared to read any complex text. For more information, check out *Why We Read What We Read* by Lisa Adams and John Heath from 2007.

I noticed that a Librarian listed on her blog that she read 103 books this year. I also noticed a forum where several people aspired to read 52 books a year—one a week. Another forum said that 42 people aspired to read over 100 books this year—about two books a week. I am not sure how many of them actually reached their goals, but it gave me an idea of what people thought was obtainable.

Anyway, I started keeping track of what I was reading when I went on an academic reading binge in 1998. I was inspired and started reading nearly anything and everything. Each new book was picked up because I wanted to research a particular author or text and those texts led me to other texts and so on.

And so my habit of keeping a running list of all the books I read began. Eventually, I undertook the daunting task of trying to list all the books I'd read before I'd started keeping track. Luckily, I remembered a good number of them, though I am sure it is not a complete list. The internet helped a great deal in tracking down exact titles and the authors of books I couldn't remember. The fact that I owned part or all of various series I'd read during my childhood also helped.

Although I read voraciously, I couldn't afford to pay for such a huge collection of books. I am very thankful that my local libraries were able to feed my hunger. I outgrew my town library as a teenager and resorted to driving a half an hour or forty-five minutes to the next town over so I could use the larger county library. Even that library lacked all the resources I needed. I was happiest, I believe, when I had access to both the county library and the university library. And what I couldn't get at their locations, I was able to use inter-library loan to get what I wanted.

As an adult, I have purchased a great many books as well. Usually I buy books I've already read, but want to re-read over and over. There is a core selection of books I've kept since childhood and will not get rid of, but over the years I've bought and sold a great many used books. While I enjoy bookstores with brand new books, I find used book stores are vital to the book lover as well. Garage Sales, Church Rummage Sales and Thrift Stores are also great places to find cheap books.

And so, even with the constant influx of books, I still own roughly a thousand books of various ages, sizes and types. I might not be inclined to let any books go, but I find that I run out of room rather quickly. When I purge, I try to get rid of books that I don't think I will ever re-read and books that are easily found at local libraries. I keep the books that are rare or difficult to find even if they aren't particularly valuable.

A large portion of my collection I've had to purchase for my classes over the years. Sometimes I would sell back textbooks to the bookstore, but the bookstore often wouldn't take back older editions or novels. Then, when I began to teach, I acquired a large selection of textbooks I used in my various classes.

Kindles and eReaders are a great invention, but I doubt they will ever completely replace physical books. Kindles and eReaders come in handy while traveling and they help with storing your favorites digitally. But it would cost me a fortune to get rid of all my books and replace them digitally. Not all my books would even be available digitally, so I will keep my book collection for now.

In any case, I came up with the idea that one could have a biography made entirely out of literature. What a person read could potentially tell you more about them than the events of their lives. That is certainly the case for people like J.R.R. Tolkien. When I meet someone new, I make an effort to study their bookshelves or ask them about their reading preferences. If you know a bit about the person and you have a good list of books they like, you can often understand them better. I look at it like a puzzle and imagine myself a sort of Sherlock Holmes. My observations have provided valuable insight at times.

I am not sure what one would glean from this comprehensive list other than the fact that I love to read. I have a variety of interests and tastes. I read in nearly every genre, as I write in nearly every genre. Sometimes I prefer nonfiction, but a lot of times I enjoy good fiction. I don't distinguish between fun and easy beach reads or difficult and complex academic texts, as I think they both are important and have their place in the world.

One of my favorite theories is that of Intertextuality. It says that anything we've ever read gets poured into our writing. That means potentially we are all part of a neverending story. A long list of books went into our favorite books, which, in turn, goes into our own reading and writing. We interpret what we read through the lens of all the other literature we've been exposed to and this makes each reading somewhat unique. Reader response says that the text itself isn't complete until we, the reader, are there to complete it. Authors give the books life, but the readers make that life their own and make the stories immortal.

This long list of books will continue to give my favorite authors and their texts life. It will also give their work and my own life a sort of immortality.

The Wonderful Wizard of Oz
The Marvelous Land of Oz
Ozma of Oz
Dorothy and the Wizard in Oz
The Road To Oz
The Emerald City of Oz
The Patchwork Girl of Oz
Rink-A-Tink in Oz
Tic-Tock of Oz
The Scarecrow of Oz
The Tinwoodman of Oz
The Lost Princess of Oz
The Magic of Oz
Glinda of Oz

The Lion, The Witch and The Wardrobe
Prince Caspian
The Voyage of the Dawn Treader
A Horse and His Boy
The Silver Chair
The Magician's Nephew
The Last Battle

Blue Fairy Book (1889)
Green Fairy Book (1890)
Red Fairy Book (1892)
Yellow Fairy Book (1894)
Grey Fairy Book (1900)
Pink Fairy Book (1897)
Crimson Fairy Book (1903)
Brown Fairy Book (1904)
Orange Fairy Book (1906)
Olive Fairy Book (1907)
Lilac Fairy Book (1910)

Wrinkle In Time
Madeline L'Engle

A Wind In The Door
Madeline L'Engle

A Swiftly Tilting Planet
Madeline L'Engle

Little House In The Big Woods
By The Shores of Silver Lake
On the Banks of Plum Creek
Little House on the Prairie
The Long Winter
Farmer Boy
These Golden Years
The First Four Years

Anne of Green Gables
Anne of Avonlea
Anne of the Island
Anne of Windy Poplars
Anne's House of Dreams
Anne of Ingleside
Rainbow Valley
Rilla of Ingleside

Stories of Avonlea
LM Montgomery

Kilmey of the Orchard
LM Montgomery

Emily of the New Moon
LM Montgomery

Emily Climbs
LM Montgomery

Emily's Quest
LM Montgomery

Donna Parker Special Agent
Donna Parker Takes A Giant Step
Donna Parker Mystery at Arawak
Donna Parker on Her Own
Donna Parker in Hollywood
Donna Parker Spring to Remember

Trixie Belden: Red Trailer Mystery
Julie Campbell

An Acceptable Time
Madeline L'Engle

The Magic Garden
Gene Stratton-Porter

The Song of The Cardinal
Gene Stratton Porter

The Circus Girl Without A Name
Wilma Pitchford Hayes

Little Women
Louisa May Alcott

Little Men
Louisa May Alcott

Jo's Boys
Louisa May Alcott

A Hidden Magic
Vivian Vande Velde

Cat's Magic ($78)
Margaret Greaves

Circle in the Sea ($55)
Steven Senn

Spacebread
Steven Senn

Casilda of the Rising Moon
Elizabeth Borden De Trevino

Island of the Blue Dolphins
Scott O'Dell

Zia
Scott O'Dell

The Captive
Scott O'Dell

The Feathered Serpent
Scott O'Dell

The Worst Witch
Jill Murphy

The Ghost in the Garden
Carol Behrman

The Forest of App
Gloria Rand Dank

My Mother The Witch
Rose Blue

The Witch Herself
Phyllis Reynolds Naylor

Witch Water
Phyllis Reynolds Naylor

The Witch Returns
Phyllis Reynolds Naylor

Witch's Sister
Phyllis Reynolds Naylor

Lizzie of Sherwood Forest
Marilyn Singer

Annabelle Starr, ESP
Lila Perl

Beyond Another Door
Sonia Levitin

The Shattered Stone
Robert Newman

Children of the Dragon
Rose Estes

Dragonsbard
Shirley Rousseau Murphy

The Ivory Lyre
Shirley Rousseau Murphy

Caddie Woodlawn
Carol Ryrie Brink

The Amethyst Ring
Scott O'Dell

The King's Fifth
Scott O'Dell

Bridge to Terabithia
Katherine Patterson

The Castle in the Attic
Elizabeth Winthrop

Me and Katie the Pest
Ann M. Martin

The Kidnapping of Anna
Ruth Hooker

The Unicorn with the Silver Shoes ($179)
Ella Young

Help, I'm A Prisoner of the Library
Eth Clifford

Tales of a Fourth Grade Nothing
Judy Blume

Nothing's fair in Fifth Grade
Barthe Declements

Sixth Grade Can Really Kill You
Barthe Declements

Tink in a Tangle
Dorothy Haas

Tread Softly
Kate Pennington

Poppy the Outdoor Cat
Dorothy Haas

Rainbow Kid
Jeanne Betancourt

Pippi Longstocking
Astrid Lindgre

Sarah Plain and Tall
Patricia MacLauchlan

Ramona the Brave
Beverly Cleary

Ramona and her Father
Beverly Cleary

Ramona the Pest
Beverly Cleary

Beezus and Ramona
Beverly Cleary

Ramona, Age 8
Beverly Cleary

Ramona and her Mother
Beverly Cleary

Ramona Forever
Beverly Cleary

Ramona's World
Beverly Cleary

Henry and the Paper Route
Beverly Cleary

Henry and the Club House
Beverly Cleary

Henry and Risby
Beverly Cleary

Socks
Beverly Cleary

Ralph the Mouse
Beverly Cleary

Follow My Leader
James B. Garfield

Heidi
Johanna Spyri

The Secret Garden
Frances Hodgson Burnett

The Little Princess
Frances Hodgson Burnett

Where The Lilies Bloom
Bill Cleaver

Where The Red Fern Grows
Wilson Rawls

Arm of the Starfish
Madeline L'Engle

A House Like A Lotus
Madeline L'Engle

The Young Unicorns
Madeline L'Engle

The Moon By Night
Madeline L'Engle

Necessary Parties
Barbara Dana

Young Joan
Barbara Dana

A Darker Magic
Michael Bedard

Alice in Wonderland
Lewis Carroll

The Little Prince
Antoine de Saint-Exupéry

The Illyrian Adventure
Lloyd Alexander

The Drackenburg Adventure
Lloyd Alexander

No Children, No Pets
Marion Holland ($67)

Shadow Castle
Marian Cockrell

Bobbsey Twins Houseboat
Laura Lee Hope

The Bobbsey Twins
Laura Lee Hope

The Wind in The Willows
Kenneth Grahame

The Witching of Ben Wagner
Sam Bottoms

Who Walks By Moonlight
Marjorie McEvoy

Circle of Time
Margaret J Anderson

Red Bird of Ireland
Sondra Green Langford

Hatchet
Gary Paulson

The Boy Who Could Fly
Robert Newman

The Reluctant God
Pamela Service

Seven Spells to Farewell
Betty Baker

Blue Willow
Doris Gates

Mystery of the Pirate Oak
Helen Fuller Orton

The Judera Adventure
Lloyd Alexander

The Magic Cup
Andrew M Greely

Willow
Wayland Drew

The Hobbit
JRR Tolkien

The Fellowship of the Ring
JRR Tolkien

The Two Towers
JRR Tolkien

The Return of the King
JRR Tolkien

The Neverending Story
Michael Ende

She Who Remembers
Linda Lay Shuler

Silverland
Nancy Harding

Bard
Morgan Lywenn

Grania
Morgan Lywenn

Druids
Morgan Lywenn

Finn McCool
Morgan Lywenn

Walks in My Soul
Lucia St. Clair Robson

Miss Pickerell Goes To Mars
Ellen MacGregor

The Goonies
James Kahn

Star Wars
George Lucas

The Empire Strikes Back
Donald Glut

The Return of the Jedi
James Kahn

Splinter of the Mind's Eye
Alan Dean Foster

Raiders of the Lost Ark
Campbell Black

The Temple of Doom
James Kahn

The Last Crusade
Rob MacGregor

Sweet Valley High Series by Francine Pascal

1. Double Love
2. Secrets
3. Playing for Keeps
4. Power Play
5. All Night Long
6. Dangerous Love
7. Dear Sister
8. Heartbreaker
9. Racing Hearts
10. Wrong Kind of Girl
11. Too Good To Be True
12. When Love Dies
13. Kidnapped!
14. Deceptions
15. Promises
16. Rags to Riches
17. Love Letters
18. Head Over Heels
19. Showdown
20. Crash Landing!
21. Runaway
22. Too Much In Love
23. Say Goodbye
24. Memories
25. Nowhere To Run
26. Hostage
27. Lovestruck
28. Alone in the Crowd
29. Bitter Rivals
30. Jealous Lies
31. Taking Sides
32. The New Jessica
33. Starting Over
34. Forbidden Love
35. Out of Control
36. Last Chance
37. Rumors
38. Leaving
39. Secret Admirer
40. On the Edge
41. Outcast
42. Caught in the Middle
43. Hard Choices
44. Pretenses

46. Decisions
47. Troublemaker
48. Slam Book Fever
49. Playing for Keeps
50. Out of Reach
51. Against the Odds
52. White Lies
53. Second Chance
54. Two Boy Weekend
62. Who's Who
64. Ghost of Tricia Martin
65. Trouble At Home
67. The Parent Plot
Spring Fever
Deadly Summer
Malibu Summer
Double Jeopardy
The Winter Carnival
The Perfect Summer
The Wakefield Legacy
A Special Christmas
On The Run

The Caitlin Series
by Francine Pascal

Loving
Love Lost
True Love

Tender Promises
Promises Broken
A New Promise

Dreams of Forever
Forever and Always
Together Forever

Blue Ribbon Series
by Chris St. John
1. Riding High
2. A Horse of Her Own
5. Time Out for Jessie

Peace Project 1990-91

A Peace Reader by Feyhe and Armstrong
A Peace Catalogue
For Peace and Justice: Pacifism in America 1914-1946
Hard Way To Peace
The Peace Reform in America
The Great Peace March
War in Peace in the Global Village
The Peace Bible

Environmentalist

The Environmental Crisis
Our Endangered Atmosphere
Our Endangered Earth
The Late Great Planet Earth
Green Life Style Handbook
The Rights of Nature
Silent Spring by Rachel Carson
Kinship with All Life

Sociology 1990-93

Sociology: A College Outline
Violence And the Family
Violence and the Media
Addiction
Straight Talk about Drugs and Alcohol
Barbiturates
Amphetamines
Preventive Parenting
Crime in Society
The Homeless Problem
Alternatives to Violence
Nuclear Power: Opposing Views
Age of Manipulation
The Conserver Society
Future Shock

Social Work 1998-99
Reviving Ophelia
Life Guards
One Girl in Ten

Swept Away
Within Our Reach
Child Welfare Report

Psychology

Psychology: A College Outline
Abnormal Psychology: A College Outline
Sigmund Freud: The Interpretation of Dreams
Sigmund Freud: New Introductory Lectures on Psycho-Analysis
The Art of Loving by Eric Fromm
About Love by Robert Solomen
Freedom and Beyond by B.F. Skinner

Self-improvement

The Idiots Guide to A Healthy Relationship by Dr. Judy
Generation Sex by Dr. Judy
Necessary Losses by Judith Voherst
Love by Leo Buscaglia
Loving Each Other by Leo Buscaglia
Living, Loving and Learning by Leo Buscaglia
All I Needed to Know I Learned in Kindergarten by Robert Fulgulm
Uh-Oh by Robert Fulgulm
It Was On Fire When I Lay Down On It by Robert Fulgulm
You Can Heal Your Life by Louise Hay
Living in the Light by Shakti Gawain
Path of Transformation by Shakti Gawain
A Return To Love by Marianne Williamson
Path of Love by Deepak Chopra
The Way of The Wizard by Deepak Chopra
Love is Letting Go Of Fear by Gerald G. Jampolsky
A Course in Love by John Gultuso
Ten Laws of Lasting Love by Paul Cearsons Phd
Handwriting Analysis
Body Language
Dream Interpretation
Scientology by L. Ron Hubbard
Dianatics by L. Ron Hubbard

New Age General

Out on a Limb by Shirley MacLaine
Dancing in the Light by Shirley MacLaine
It's all in the Playing by Shirley MacLaine
Going Within by Shirley McLaine
Ecstasy is a New Frequency by Chris Griscom

Edgar Cayce
Seven Mansions of Color by Alex Jones
You Were Meant To Be Together by Dick Sutphan
True Magic by Llweynn
Spiral Dance by Starhawk
Dreaming the Dark by Starhawk (Women Studies)
Truth or Dare by Starhawk (Women Studies)
A Women's Book of Rituals and Celebrations by Barbara Ardinger
Dance of the Spirit: Seven Steps to Women's Spirituality by Maria Harris
You Are Psychic by Peter A Sanders Jr.
The Celestine Prophecy by James Redfield (Also Fiction)
Abduction by John E Mark MD
Holy Blood Holy Grail (also Religious)

Native American

Lame Deer: Seeker of Visions
The Gospel of The Red Man
Death of The Great Spirit by Earl Shorris
Trail of Tears (Fiction)
She Who Remembers (Fiction) by Linda Lay Shuler
Woman of The Mists (Fiction)

Reincarnation

The Reincarnation Primer by Holzer
How to Uncover Your Past Lives by Andrews
Life after Life Raymond Moody
Life Cycles: Reincarnation and the Web of Life by Christopher Bach PhD
Your Past Lives by Talbot Michael
Reincarnation Workbook: Reincarnation, A New Horizon

Eastern Thought

A Path With Heart by John Kornfield
The Wisdom of Insecurity
The Looking Glass God by Nathum Stiskin
The Song of God: The Bhavagad Gita
Open Reality
The Self-Knowledge (Antambodha) Translated by Swami Nikhilands
Think on these Things by J. Krisnimirti
The Way of The Tao
The Essential Zen Buddhism
The Essential Sufism
The Meditative Mind by Daniel Goleman
Confucius
Fung Shui

The Kama Sutra
Siddahartha by Herman Hesse (Also Fiction)
Dancing Wu Li Masters (Also Science/Tech)

Philosophy

Plato: Dialogues
Birth of Tragedy by Nietezche
Being and Nothingness by Sartre
(See List for May 1998-March 1999)
Loneliness in Philosophy and Literature
Rousse, Kant and Goethe
The Meaning of Teilhard De Chardin
What do we Mean when we say God? by Deidre Sullivan

History

In Search of The Maya by Robert Brunhouse
Plotting Hitler's Death by Joachim Fest
The Incas
The Aztecs
The Life of The Celts
The Dead Sea Scrolls (3 books)

Bio/Lit Criticism

G.B. Shaw
Chekhov
Edgar Allen Poe
Dorothy Parker
Ruth Hall
Ondaatje
Jim Harrison
Anne Rice
L.M. Montgomery
L Frank Baum
C.S. Lewis

Professor's Books

Transformation and Texts by Steven Joyce
Desire, The Self and The Social Critic by J.F. Buckley
Anne Finch by McGovern
Clash of Civilizations by Burke
Environmentalism in Germany by Dominic

Literature

Essays on Transcendentalism
(See May 1998-March 1999 List)

Biography/Autobiography

Tobias Wolf--This Boys Life
Mary Karr--Liars Club
Katherine Harris--The Kiss
Michael Ondaatje--Running in The Family
Joyce Carol Oates--The Invisible Writer
Conversations with Joyce Carol Oats
Conversation with Anne Rice
Bram Stoker
The Bronte's--A Life in Letters
Shaw--Definitive Edition
Louisa May Alcott
Anne Morrow Lindbergh (paper)
Josephine Baker (paper)
Ma Rainy and Bessie Smith (paper)
Mary Tyler Moore--After All
Charlie Chaplin
George Lucas--SkyWalking
Steven Spielberg
David Duchovany
Gillian Anderson
Mariah Carey
Mark-Paul Gosselaar
River Phoenix
Brad Pitt
Melissa Ethridge
Janis Joplin--Love Janis
Doors--Nobody Gets out of Hear Alive
Jim and Pamela Morrison--Angels Dance and Angels Die
Ray Manzarik--Light My Fire
Trent Reznor--NIN
Marilyn Manson--The long road out of Hell
Dolly Parton
Whitney Houston--Diva
Brett Butler--Knee Deep in Paradise
Tim Allen--Don't Stand too Close to a Naked Man
Ellen DeGeneres--And I Do Have a Point
Seinfeld--Sienlangue
Paul Riser--Couplehood
Whoopi Goldberg--Book

High School

Romeo and Juliet
Julius Cesar
Macbeth
Hamlet
Moby Dick
Poe's Poetry
Cask of Amontillado
Last of the Mohicans
Young Goodman Brown
Alcott's Character Sketches
Walden
Walt Whitman's Leaves of Grass

American Literature to 1865

John Winthrop
Anne Bradstreet
Samuel Sewall
Jonathan Edwards
Benjamin Franklin
Wieland by Brown
Thomas Jefferson
Appeal by Walker
Emerson
Margaret Fuller
Ruth Hall by Fannie Fern
Poe
Rebecca Harding Davis
Walt Whitman
Emily Dickinson

French Literature

Princess de Cleves
Candide
Eugene Grandet
The Red and the Black
No Exit and Other Plays
Proust (Excerpt)

British Literature

Canterbury Tales
King Lear
Milton's Paradise Lost
Gulliver's Travels
Alexander Pope
Ben Johnson's Rasselas
Wordsworth
Coleridge
Keats
Dickens Great Expectations
Robert Browning
Conrad's Heart of Darkness
Yeats
D.H. Lawrence
Samuel Beckett
Doris Lessing

Shakespeare

Titus Andronicus
Taming of the Shrew
Midsummer Night's Dream
Henry IV Part 1
Henry IV Part 2
Hamlet
The Tempest

Critical Writing

Dorothy Parker
Shirley Jackson
King Lear
John Updike
William Faulkner
Nathaniel Hawthorn
Edgar Alan Poe

Intro To Poetry

Whitman
Dorothy Parker
Theodore Roethke
Percy Bryce Shelly
Andrew Marvel
Adrianne Rich
Emily Dickinson
W.H. Auden
Shakespeare's Sonnets
Robert Frost
N Scott Momaday
Sylvia Plath
Elizabeth Barret Browning
William Blake
Keats
Anne Sexton
Carolyn Forche
Robert Hass
William Carlos Williams

Modern Drama

Ibsen
Chekov
Strindberg
Schnitzler
Wilde
Synge
Shaw
Nietzsche

Post-Colonial Literature

Heat and Dust by Jhavala
Things Fall Apart by Achebe
Reservation Blues by Sherman Alexie
The Holder of the World Mukherjee
House the Spirits by Isabelle Allende

Film Studies

Occurrence At Owl Creek
Wuthering Heights
Dracula by Bram Stoker
Death in Venice by Mann
The English Patient

Introduction To Fiction

Edgar Alan Poe
Turn of the Screw
Sherlock Holmes
Haunting of Hill House
Joyce Carol Oates

Fiction Books I Read 1990-1998

The Bodyguard
Lawrence Kasaden

My Girl
Patricia Hermes

The Good Son
Tad Strasser & Ian McIwan

Far and Away
Sonja Massie

Beaches
Iris Rainer Dart

The Prince of Tides
Pat Conroy

Basic Instinct
Richard Osborne

Sliver
Ira Levin

Fatal Attraction
H.B. Gilmore

A League of Their Own
Sara Gilbert

Shoeless Joe Jackson
W.P Kinsella

Romancing The Stone
Joan Wilder

Jewel of the Nile
Joan Wilder

Nell
Mary Ann Evans

Dances with Wolves
William Blake

Woman of the Mists
Lynn Armistead McKee

Keeper of Dreams
Lynn Armistead McKee

Walks in Stardust
Lynn Armistead McKee

Touches the Stars
Lynn Armistead McKee

Voice of the Eagle
Linda Lay Shuler

Sound of the Drum
Linda Lay Shuler

Ice and Rapture
Connie Mason

Brave Land Brave Love
Connie Mason

Gentle Rogue
Johanna Lindsey

Once a Princess
Johanna Lindsay

Prisoner of My Desire
Johanna Lindsey

Surrender My Love
Johanna Lindsey

Savage Thunder
Johanna Lindsey

Angel
Johanna Lindsey

Surrender
Emily Carmichael

Thunderheart
Lowell Charters

Braveheart
Randle Wallace

Postcards from the Edge
Carrie Fischer

Home for the Holidays
Chris Radent

Quantum Leap Too Close For Comfort
Ashley McConnell

Magic Kingdom for Sale Sold
Terry Brooks

The Black Unicorn
Terry Brooks

Wizard at Large
Terry Brooks

Fools
Pat Cadigan

Virtual Mode
Piece Anthony

Encounters at Farpoint
David Gerrold

Q-In-Law
Peter David

Imzadi
Peter David

Imzadi Forever
Peter David

The Vampire Diaries: The Awakening
LJ Smith

A Time to Kill
John Grisham

The Firm
John Grisham

The Pelican Brief
John Grisham

Search the Shadows
Barbara Michaels

Wait for What Will Come
Barbara Michaels

The Sphinx
Robin Cook

Rising Sun
Michael Crichton

Presumed Innocent
Scott Turow

Zoya
Danielle Steele

Secrets
Danielle Steele

Kaleidoscope
Danielle Steele

The Dark Angel
Meredith Pierce

A Gathering of Gargoyles
Meredith Pierce

Wish You a Merry Murder
Valerie Wolzien

Vampire Diaries: The Fury
LJ Smith

The Vampire Diaries: The Struggle
LJ Smith

Light a Single Candle
Beverly Butler

The Way We Were
Arthur Laurents

A Time To Choose
Janine Boissard

A Matter of Feeling
Janine Boissard

Acts of Love
Maureen Daly

Indiana Jones and the Peril at Delphi
Rob MacGregor

Indian Jones and the Dance of the Giants
Rob MacGregor

Indiana Jones and the Seven Veils
Rob MacGregor

Indiana Jones and the Genesis Deluge
Rob MacGregor

Indiana Jones and the Unicorn's Legacy
Rob MacGregor

Indiana Jones and the Interior World
Rob MacGregor

Indiana Jones and the White Witch
Martin Cadin

Exit to Eden
Anne Rice

Cry To Heaven
Anne Rice

Prism of the Night
Katherine Ramsland

Vampire Diaries: Reunion
LJ Smith

Heartbeats
Norma Mazer

Just Friends
Norma Klein

It's Ok if You Don't Love
Norma Klein

No More Saturday Nights
Norma Klein

Prince of Thieves
Simon Green

Interview with a Vampire
Anne Rice

Lestat the Vampire
Anne Rice

Queen of the Damned
Anne Rice

Tale of the Body Thief
Anne Rice

Memnoch the Devil
Anne Rice

The Mummy
Anne Rice

Belinda
Anne Rice

Claiming of Sleeping Beauty
Anne Rice

Armand the Vampire
Anne Rice

Violin
Anne Rice

Vittorio The Vampire
Anne Rice

Rush
Kim Wozencraft

Conspiracy Theory
J.H. Marks

The X-Files Ground Zero
Kevin J Anderson

The X-Files Whirlwind
Charles Grant

The X-Files Antibodies
Kevin J Anderson

Fight the Future
Elizabeth Hand

Iona Moon
Melanie Rae Thon

Angels and Insects
A.S. Byatt

Lizard
Banana Yoshimoto

Kitchen
Banana Yoshimoto

Amrita
Banana Yoshimoto

Red Azalea
Anchee Min

Katherine
Anchee Min

Joy Luck Club
Amy Tan

Pandora
Anne Rice

Sleepers
Lorenzo Carcaterra

Bridges of Madison County
James Waller

Legends of the Fall
Jim Harrison

Exposure
Katherine Harrison

Damage
Josephine Hart

Sin
Josephine Hart

The Stillest Day
Josephine Hart

Eyes of the Night
Diane Bane

Wild Promise, Sweet Promise
Janelle Taylor

Last Viking Queen
Janelle Taylor

The Power of One
Bruce Courteney

Like Water For Chocolate
Laura Esquivel

Holder of the World
Bharati Mukherjee

Heat and Dust
Ruth Prowler Jhabvala

House of the Spirits
Isabelle Allande

Reservation Blues
Sherman Alexi

Night Magic
Charlotte Van Allen

Heir to the Empire
Timothy Zahn

The Story of O
Pauline Reage

Dharma Bums
Jack Kerouac

Foxfire
Joyce Carol Oates

The Princess De Cleves
Madame de Lafayette

Eugene Gannet
Honore de Balzac

The Hottest State
Ethan Hawk

The Last Unicorn
Peter S Beagle

Wuthering Heights
Emily Bronte

Dracula
Bram Stoker

Death in Venice
Thomas Mann

The English Patient
Michael Ondaatje

Solo Variations
Cassandra Garbus

Fall of Sparrow
Robert Helgna

Dracula
James V Hart

Shadow Moon
Chris Claremont

Walden
Henry David Thoreau

Quiet on the Western Front
Erich Maria Remarque

Haunted
Joyce Carol Oates

Candide
Voltaire

The Red and the Black
Stendhal

Lord of the Flies
William Golden

Things Fall Apart
Chinua Achebe

Hunchback of Notre Dame
Victor Hugo

Phantom of the Opera
Gaston LeRoux

To Kill A Mockingbird
Harper Lee

Leaves of Grass
Walt Whitman

Reading List
May 1999 to July 2000

A Path with Heart
Jack Kornfield

Bernard Shaw Bio
Holroyd

A Movable Feast
Ernest Hemingway

Theses on Wings of Desire

Beyond Another Door
Sonia Levin

Lolita
Nabokov

Animal Farm
George Orwell

The Sound and the Fury
William Faulkner

All the Pretty Horses
McCormack

Notebook
Nickolas Sparks

The Awakening
Kate Chopin

An Ocean in Iowa
Peter Hedges

Solo Variations
Casandra Garbus

A Farewell to Arms
Hemmingway

The Philosophy of Hegel

Fall of A Sparrow
Robert Helenga

Inner Revolution
Robert Thurman

At Close Range
Annie Proulx

Letters by Tipen

Delta of Venus
Anais Nin

A Spy in the House of Love
Anais Nin

White Stains
Anais & Friend

Little Birds
Anais Nin

Diaries of Anais Nin Vol 1-7

Anais Nin Reader

Unbearable Lightness of Being
Milan Kundra

Immortality
Milan Kundra

Proust: Penguin Life Series

Swann's Way
Marcel Proust

How to Read a Poem

Book of Love (Collection)

The Brothers
Dostoyevsky

Kant

Bio of Anais Nin
Deidre Blaire

Cities of the Interiors
Anais Nin

Winter of the Artifice
Anais Nin

Under the Glass Bell
Anais Nin

Novel of the Future
Anais Nin

Collages
Anais Nin

Early Diary of Anais Nin Vol 2
Anais Nin

Henry and June
Anais Nin

Journal of Incest
Anais Nin

Journal of Fire
Anais Nin

Nearer to the Moon
Anais Nin

Interview with Anais

In Favor of the Sensitive Man
Anais Nin

Unprofessional Study of Lawrence
Anais Nin

Existence and Being
Heidegger

Local Girls
Alice Hoffmann

Selected letters and Poems
Veronica Franco

The Witch Must Die
Sheldon Cashdan

Zen and the Art of Motorcycle Maintenance

World as Will and Representation
Schopenhauer

Moll Flanders
Defoe

Tropic of Cancer
Henry Miller

Anna Karenna
by Tolstoy

On the Road
by Kerouac

Piercing the Darkness (Vampires)
Katherine Ramsland

Masks of the Gods 1-4
Campbell

Mythmaker
John Baxter (About George Lucas)

Hero with a Thousand Faces
Joseph Campbell

The Old Man and the Sea
Ernest Hemmingway

Reflections
Carl G Jung

Girl Interrupted
Susana Kaysen

Djuana Barnes Reader

Henry Miller Reader

Poems by Jim Carroll

Topic of Capricorn
Henry Miller

The Genius of Affection
Marilyn Sides

A Woman Speaks
Anais Nin

Collected Works
Flannery O'Conner

Conversations of God 1-3
Neale Walsh

Collector of Hearts
Joyce Carol Oates

Yoga and the Quest/True Self
Stephan Cope

The Island of The Mapmaker's Wife
Marilyn Sides

Wars and Peace (Family Memoir)
Rory Quick

Night Falls Fast
Kay Redfield Jamieson

Crooked Little Heart
Anne Lamott

The Cities of The Ancient Andes
Hagen and Morris

The Feast (Translated)
Randy Lee Eickhoff

The Good Part
Erotica Anthology

Yellow Silk
Ed. Lily Pond

Far Afield
Susana Kaysen

Where I've Been...
Joyce Carol Oates

The User Illusion: Consciousness
Tor Norretranders

Waste of Timelessness
Anais Nin

Best Short Stories of 1999
Ed. Amy Tan

Jasmine
Bharati Mukherjee

The Kind I'm Likely to Get
Ken Foster

Harry Potter: Sorcerer's Stone
R.L. Rowling

Map of the World
Jane Hamilton

Snow Falling on Cedars
David Gutterson

The Science Behind The X-Files
Anne Simon, Ph.D.

Island of Women and Amazons
Betya Wienbaum

When The Kissing Had to Stop...
John Leonard

Think
Simon Blackburn

Angela's Ashes
Frank McCourt

The Seat of The Soul
Gary Zukav

Best Short Stories
of the Century

The Myth of Sisyphus
Camus

New Stories from the South 1999

The Lion in the Room Next Door
Merilyn Simonds

What Remains
By Christa Wolf

Three Plays Translated
Fredrich C. Hebbel

Where the Heart Is
Billie Letts

Studies in the Lyrical Poems of Hebbel
Gubelmann

Fredrich Hebbel
Purdie

Hebbel as A Dramatic Artist
Rees

Going Home:
Thich Nhat Hanh

How to Know God
Deepak Chopra

Cybil Disobedience
Cybil Shepherd

In the Gloaming
Alice Elliot Dark

American's Favorite Poems
Ed. Robert Pinsky

The Existential Imagination
Frederick M. Karl

Psychoanalysis and Literature
Hendrick M. Ruitenbeek

Cassandra's Daughter:
Joseph Schwartz

Play It As It Lays
Joan Didion

The Last Thing He Wanted
Joan Didion

Essays & Conversations
With Joan Didion/ Ed. Friedman

A Common Prayer
Joan Didion

Run River
Joan Didion

Anil's Ghost
Michael Ondaatje

The Camino
Shirley MacLaine

After Ecstasy, The Laundry
Jack Kornfield

Tuesday's With Morrie
Mitch Albom

Anais Nin
Bettina Knapp

Sparks of Genius
Root-Bernstein

Anatomy of the Spirit
Carolyn Myss

How to Read and Why
Harold Bloom

End of the Affair
Graham Greene

Love Poems
Anne Sexton

Women and Desire
Polly Young-Eisendrath

Women, Myth & Feminine Principle
Bettina Knapp

Dream and Image
Bettina Knapp

Exile and the Writer
Bettina Knapp

Literature as Exploration
Louise M. Rosenblatt

If On A Winter's Night A Traveler
Italo Calvino

Yellow Silk II
Pond

Reading List
August 2000—July 2001

The Perfect Storm
Junger

Life with Monte Cisco
Bio of Eugene O'Neill

Bless the Child
Catherine Cash Spellman

Sons and Lovers (class)
D.H. Lawrence

The Rainbow (class)
D.H. Lawrence

Women in Love (class)
D.H. Lawrence

Lady Chatterley's Lover
D.H. Lawrence

Complete Short Stories (V2)
D.H. Lawrence

Lawrence's Literary Inheritors
Ed. Cushman and Jackson

The Challenge of D.H. Lawrence
Ed. Sequres and Cushman

Phoenix: Posthumous Paper of DHL
Collected by

Lawrence Among the Women
Carol Siegle

Anais: The Erotic Life of Anais Nin
Noel Riley Fitch

The Mirror and the Garden
Hinz

Anais Nin And Her Critics
Philip K. Jason

To The Other Side And Back
Sylvia Browne

One Dark Night
Kathleen Blease

Chasing Down the Dawn
Jewel

On Writing
Stephen King

A Haunted House (class)
Virginia Woolf

Jacob's Room (class)
Virginia Woolf

In the Presence of the Sun
N. Scott Momaday

Angle of Geese (Poems)
M. Scott Momaday

Anais Nin: An Intro.
Benjamin Franklin V

Collage of Dreams
Spencer (About Nin)

Anais Nin: Remaking Self
Richard-Allerdyce

Anais Nin
Oliver Evens

The Hours
Michael Cunningham

Merrick
Anne Rice

Mansfield: A Town In The Wilderness
Levison

Coffinberry Genealogy

Mrs. Dalloway (class)
Virginia Woolf

To The Lighthouse (class)
Virginia Woolf

Orlando (class)
Virginia Woolf

The Wounded Daughter
Leonard

Cherry
Mary Karr

The World without A Self
James Naremore

Virginia Woolf
Michael Rosenthal

Virginia Woolf: A Critical Heritage
Robin Majumder

Virginia Woolf and PM
Pamela L. Caughie

Dark City
Frank Lauria

The Body Artist
Don Dellio

Psychoanalysis in Shpke
Norman N. Holland

Medea
Christa Wolf

The House of Sand and Fog
Andre Dubus III

Gravity
Tess Gerritison

Have and Have Nots
Ed. Barbara Solomon

Slut: Bad Reputation
Lenora Tannenbaum

Aqua Erotica
Ed. Mary Anne Mohanraj

Four Agreements
Miguel Ruiz

Indestructible Truth:
Reginald A. Ray

Information Anxiety 2
Richard Saul Wurman

Psychology Everyday Things
Donald A. Norman

Plato's Cratylus
Translated by C.D.C Reeve

Shakespearean Negotiations
Stephen Greenblat

Advice from an Old Mistress
As Told To Michael Drury

Antony and Cleo
Shakespeare

Coriolanus
Shakespeare

Common Liar
Jane Alderman

Ego and Archetype
Edward Endinger

Narrating PM Time and Space
Joseph Francese

Italo Calvino
Martin McLaughin

Under The Radiant Sun
Angela M. Jeannet

Calvino: Neorealism
Lucia Re

Understanding Calvino
Beno Weiss

The Virgin Suicides
Jeffery Eugenides

King Lear (class)
Shakespeare

The Dutch Courtesan (class)
Marston

Macbeth (class)
Shakespeare

The Revenger's Tragedy
Middleton

Thinking the Difference
Irigaray

The Perfect Crime
Baudrillard

Herland and Other Stories
Charlotte Perkins Gilman

Pages for You
Sylvia Brownrigg

Philaster
Beaumont &Fletcher

Pericles
Shakespeare

Epicoene
Jonson

The Alchemist
Jonson

A Winter's Tale
Shakespeare

The Tempest
Shakespeare

Texts and Hypertexts
Gaggi

Hypertext 2.0
Lando

Act of Reading
Wolfgang Iser

Reader-Response
Ed. Jane Tompkins

Ficcones
Borges

If You Meet Buddha
Sheldon B. Knopp

Tropic of Orange
Karen Tei Yamashita

The Art of the Novel
Milan Kundera

Writing about Fiction
William Kenney

A Course in Miracles
Foundation for Peace

Tropic Of Cancer
Henry Miller

Absalom, Absalom
William Faulkner

Juneteenth
Ralph Ellison

Herzog
Saul Bellow

Miller: Paris Years
Gilberte Brassai

Henry Miller On Writing
Ed. Thomas H. Moore

Henry Miller's Letters To Anais Nin
Edited by Gunther Stuhlmann

A Literate Passion
Letters of Miller and Nin

Significant Others
by Chadwick and De Courtivrons

Notes on Aaron's Rod
by Henry Miller

Tariki: Discovering Peace
Hiroyuki Itsuki

Gothic: 400 years of…
Richard Davenport-Hienes

Heathcliff's Journey Back
Lin Haire Sergeant

Scott O'Dell
Twayne Publishers

Madonna
J. Randy Taraborrelli

Dune
Frank Herbert

Mists of Avalon
Marion Zimmer Bradley

Reading List August
2002—August 2003

The Myth of Monogamy
David Barrish, PhD

Woman: An Intimate Geography
Natalie Angier

Making Babies
David Bainbridge

Fear of Flying (Again)
Erica Jong

Amy and Isabelle
Elizabeth Strout

Enders Game
Orson Scott Card

Good in Bed
Elizabeth Warner

The Time Machine
H.G. Wells

The Idiot Girls' Action Adventure
Club—by Laurie Notaro

Catcher in the Rye
J.D. Salinger

Sacred Contracts
Caroline Myss

Trail Feathers
(Inca Birdmen)

9 Steps to Financial Freedom
Suzie Orman

Gold of Cuzco
A.B. Daniels

Sexus
Henry Miller

Surfacing
Margaret Atwood

The Shadow of the Puma
A.B. Daniel

The Fury (Again)
L.J. Smith

The Struggle (Again)
L.J. Smith

Big Trouble
Dave Berry

Alias: Recruited
Mason

Medea (Again)
Christa Wolf

Room For One More
Anna Perrott Rose

Ignorance
Milan Kundra

The Alchemist
Paul Coehelo

Are You Ready For Lasting
Love? By Paddy Wells PhD

Genius
Harold Bloom

The Secret Life of Bees
Sue Monk Kidd

Vision of Sugar Plums
Janet Evanovich

The Mammoth Hunters
Jean M. Auel

Niblenungenlied
Penguin Classics

Feathered Serpent
Colin Falconer

Midnight in the Ruby Bayou
Elizabeth Lowell

My Sister The Moon
Sue Harrison

The Sea People
Charlotte Prentiss

Mothers Who Think
Camille Peri and Kate Moses

A Good Man is Hard to Find
Flannery O'Connor

Otherwise Engaged
Susan Finnamore

Living, Loving and Learning
Leo Buscaglia

Ellen Foster
Kay Gibbons

Infant Massage
Vimala Schneider McClure

You Live, You Learn
Biography of Alanis Morrisette

Sacred Journey of the Peaceful Warrior
Dan Millman

Chakra Therapy
Sherwood

Sylvia Browne's Book
of Dreams

Any Women's Blues (Again)
Erica Jong

A Woman Speaks (Again)
Anais Nin

Memoirs of Geisha
Arthur Golden

Kitchen God's Wife
Amy Tan

The Dance of Anger
Harriet Lerner

What to Expect....
Eisenberg, Murkoff,

Nighttime Parenting
William Sears, MD

The Wisdom of the Sands
Saint Exupery

Philip K. Dick
Minority Report

The Rest of Life
Mary Gordon

Poisonwood Bible
Barbara Kingsolver

Women and Fatigue
Holly Atkinson

Into Thin Air
Jon Krakauer

Women: A Feminist
Perspective by Freeman

Lesbian Words: State of the
Art Edited by Randy Turoff

READING LIST
October 2003—August 2004

A Journey to the Center of the Earth
Jules Vern

Point of Origin
Patricia Cornwall

Into Thin Air
Jon Krakow

The Road Less Traveled
Scott M. Peck

Cultural Literacy
Ed Hirsch, J.R.

Family Pictures
Sue Miller

LOTR: Return of The King
J.R.R. Tolkien

To The Nines
Janet Evanovich

Harry Potter and the
Order of the Phoenix
J.K. Rowling

Call Me Anna
Patty Duke Story

Shopgirl
Steve Martin

Blue Shoe
Anne Lamott

Sappho's Leap
Erica Jong

How to Save Your Own Life
Erica Jong

Eros of Parenthood
Oxonhandler

Elegant Universe
Brian Greene

A Kiss of Shadows
Laurel K. Hamilton

Under the Tuscan Sun
Frances Mayes

The Nursing Mother's
Problem Solver
Claire Martin

The Earth, My Butt and
Other Round Things
Carolyn Mackler

The Gospel According
To Tolkien
Ralph C. Wood

Power of Now
Eckhart Tolle

Einstein Didn't Use
Flash Cards

Tuck Everlasting
Natalie Babbitt

Out on A Leash
Shirley McLaine

Alias: Free Fall
Christina Mason

Alias: Father Figure
Laura Peyton Roberts

Parachutes & Kisses
Erica Jong

Bird by Bird
Anne Lamott

Operating Instructions
Anne Lamott

Fear of Fifty
Erica Jong

Fanny Hackabout Jones
Erica Jong

Hard Laughter
Anne Lamott

Anais Nin, Fictionality + Femininity
Helen Tookey

Journals of Sylvia Plath
Edited by Ted Hughes

Giving Up: Last Days of Sylvia Plath
Jillian Baker

Rough Magic: Bio Sylvia Plath
Paul Alexander

Anais Nin: Literary Perspectives
Ed Suzanne Nalbantian

Seven Daughters of Eve
Bryan Sykes

Three To Get Deadly
Janet Evanovich

Four To Score
Janet Evanovich

High Five
Janet Evanovich

Seven Up
Janet Evanovich

Alias: Close Quarters
Emma Harris

Alias: Sister Spy
Laura Peyton Roberts

No Back Up
Rosemary

Wrinkle in Time (Again)
Madeline L'Engle

Alias: The Pursuit
Michael Vaughn Novel

The Dark Nights of The Soul
Thomas Moore

In The Cut
Susanna Moore

Julia Roberts: Her Life
James Spader

The Last Ride (The Missing)
Tom Eidson

My Lucky Stars (Again)
Shirley McLaine

One for the Money
Janet Evanovich

Two For the Dough
Janet Evanovich

Angels and Demons
Dan Brown

Di Vinci Code
Dan Brown

Life After Birth
Kate Figs/ Jean Zimmerman

7 Stages of Motherhood
Ann Pleshette Murphy

Hard Eight
Janet Evanovich

Ten Big Ones
Janet Evanovich

Living By Fiction (Again)
Anne Dillard

Undressing the Moon
T. Greenwood

Reading List 2005

Lemony Snicket's "A Series of Unfortunate Events"

Bad Beginnings
The Reptile Room
The Wide Window
The Miserable Mill
The Austere Academy
The Vile Village
The Ersatz Elevator
The Hostile Hospital
The Carnivorous Carnival
The Slippery Slope
The Grim Grotto
The Penultimate Peril

Modern Manors
PJ O'Rourke

Generation of Swine
Hunter S Thompson

How I Became Stupid
Martin Page

Alias: Shadowed
Lizzie Skurnick

The Nursing Mother's Companion
Kathleen Huggins RN, MS

Naked
David Sedaris

Many Waters (Again)
Madeline L'Engle

Hitchhiker's Guide to the Galaxy
Douglas Adams

Blowing My Cover: Life As An Undercover
CIA Agent: Lindsey Moran

A Kiss of Shadows (Again)
Lauren K. Hamilton

How To Expand Love
Dalia Lama

A Caress of Twilight
Laurel K. Hamilton

Seduced By Moonlight
Lauren K. Hamilton

A Stroke of Midnight
Laurel K. Hamilton

A Dark Muse: The History of the Occult
Gary Lachman

Envy
Katherine Harrison

On Bullshit
Harry G. Frankfurt

Get Me Out Of Here
Rachel Reiland

Genuine Happiness
B. Alan Wallace

The Myth of Monogamy (Again)
Barish and Lipton

Silent Bob Speaks
Writings of Kevin Smith

Secret World of Toddlers

Deep Simplicity (Chaos)
John Gribbin

Pages For You (Again)
Sylvia Brownrigg

Mother Tongue
Bill Bryson

Surfacing
Margaret Atwood

Best Buddhist Writing
2004

Marriage: A History
Stephanie Coontz

Against Depression
Peter D. Kramer

If Only: Regret
Neal Roese, PhD

The Unquiet Mind
Kay Jamieson

Poetry Repair Manual
Ted Kooser

Physics of Consciousness
Walker (Again)

User Illusion
Norretranders (Again)

Universe Single Atom
Dalia Lama

Harry Potter and the Order
of the Phoenix (Again)

Harry Potter and The Chamber
of Secrets by J.K. Rowling

Kabbalah (Beliefnet Guide To)
Arthur Goldwag

It's Up To You (Buddhism)
Dzigar Kongrtrul

Llewellyn's Magical Almanac

K.I.S.S. Yoga
Shakta Kaur Khalsa

Long Fatal Love Chase
Louisa May Alcott

Dancing Swan
Joel Schwan

Harry Potter: Half-Blood Prince
J.K. Rowling

Lion, Witch, Wardrobe
C.S. Lewis

Best American Short Stories
Of 2005

The Friend Who Got Away
Edited by Offill and Shappell

Evolutionary Witchcraft
T. Thorne Coyle

Mind Wide Open
Steve Johnson

Revenge of the Sith
Mathew Stover

Wizards
John Matthews

Self Help, INC
Micki MaGee

Walking Through The
Wardrobe by Sarah Arthur

The Sex Doctors in the
Basement by Molly Jong-Fast

Spirit of the Witch
Raven Grimassi

Sacred Selfishness
Bud Harris, Ph.D.

The Hero With A Thousand Faces
Joseph Campbell (Again)

A Short History of Myth
Karen Armstrong

The Dissident Daughter
Sue Monk Kidd

Sham
Steve Salereno

Susana's Diary for Nicholas
James Patterson

On the Kabbalah and its Symbolism
Gershome Scholem

Indiana Jones and the Peril at Delphi
Rob MacGregor

Indian Jones and the Dance of the Giants
Rob MacGregor

Indiana Jones and the Seven Veils
Rob MacGregor

Indiana Jones and the Genesis Deluge
Rob MacGregor

Indiana Jones and the Unicorn's Legacy
Rob MacGregor

Indiana Jones and the Interior World
Rob MacGregor

Willow (Again)
Wayland Drew

Dark Lord (Star Wars)
James Luceno

The Woman in the Shaman's Body
Barbara Tedlock PhD

Mystery of Reincarnation
J. Allen Danelek

The Mothman Prophecies (Again)
John Keel

Darkangel
Meredith Pierce

Dragonsbane
Barbara Hambly

Madam Bovary's Ovaries
David P. Barash

Rational Mysticism
John Hogan

The Infinite Book
John D. Barrow

How To Spot a Liar
Gregory Hartley

Banishing Verona
Margot Livesey

The Jane Austin Book Club
Karen Joy Fowler

The Goddess and the Bull
Michael Balter

Science and Sensibility
Keith J Laidler

A Day in This Life
Janie Cole

Misconceptions
Naomi Wolf

Strapped
Tamara Draut

Nickel and Dimed
Barbara Ehenreich

Bait and Switch
Barbara Ehenreich

The Family Tree
Caldwell

The Box Children
Sharron Wyse

The Lathe of Heaven
Ursula K. Le Guin

Watership Down
Richard Adams

Lancelot
Walker Percy

The Wonderful Wizard of Oz
L. Frank Baum

Not In Kansas Anymore
Christine Wicker

Are You There God? It's Me, Margaret
Judy Blume

A Land of Two Halves
Joe Bennett

Light on Life
B.K.S. Iyengar

Romancing the Buddha
Michael Lisagor

Weight
Jeanette Winterson

The Real Lemony Snicket
Haley Mitchell Haugen

Aphrodite in Jeans
Katherine Shirek Douglas

Dinner with Anna Karenina
Gloria Goldreich

Summerhouse, Later
Judith Hermann

Teacher Man
Frank McCourt

Reading Lolita in Tehran
Azar Nafisi

Archangels and Ascended Masters
Doreen Virtue, PhD

Wicca's Charm
Catherine Edwards Sanders

Readings On J.K. Rowling
Greenhouse Literary Companion

LOTR: The Myth of Power
Jane Chance

Is He Depressed Or What?
David Wexler

Eragon
Christopher Palolini

The Penelopiad
Margaret Atwood

Go Ask Orgre
Jolene Siana

Birthday Letters
Ted Hughes

Ariel's Gift
Erica Wagner

The Forgiveness Formula
Kathleen Griffin

Happiness
Daniel Nettle

Statements
Amy Borkowsky

Best American Poetry
2006

Bad Twin
Gary Troup

Our Mutual Friend
Anymore
Charles Dickens

Remembered Rapture
Bell Hooks

Writing Down the Bones

Fool's Paradise
Stewart Justman

The Road to the Dark Tower
Ben Vincent

The Gunslinger
Stephen King

The Drawing of the Three
Stephen King

The Wastelands
Stephen King

Wizard and Glass
Stephen King

Wolves of Calla
Stephen King

Susannah's Song
Stephen King

The Dark Tower
Stephen King

Rousseau: A Restless Genius
Leo Damrosch

Virginia Woolf: An Inner Life
Julia Briggs

The Making of A Philosopher
Colin McGinn

Island
Aldous Huxley

You Don't Have To Take It

Steven Stosny, PhD

Twelve Sharp
Janet Evanovich

Adverbs
Daniel Handler

Before: Shorts About Pregnancy
Emily Franklin and Heather Swain

Aspects of the Novel
E.M. Forster

Owl and Moon Cafe
Jo-Ann Mapson

Life Happens
Connie Schultz

Late Wife: Pulitzer Prize Poems
Claudia Emerson

Gnosticism: Beliefnet Guide
Richard Valantasis

More Readings on TLOTR
Robert Eaglestone

Unauthorized Guide To Lost
Lynnette Porter and David Lavery

Hearts in Atlantis
Stephen King

Loving Chloe
Jo An Mapson

Fall of A Sparrow (Again)
Robert Helenga

Life of David Gale
Dewey Gram

In the Shadow of the Ark
Anne Provoost

The Street Smart Writer
J. Glatzer and D. Steven

Generation Me
Jean M. Twenge, PhD.

78 Reasons…14 Reasons
Pat Walsh

Exploring Reality
John Polkinghorne

The Oracle
William J. Broad

The Language of God
Francis S Collins

The Last Street before Cleveland
An Accidental Pilgrimage
Joe MacKall

Briar Rose
Jane Yolen

The Sun Also Rises
Ernest Hemingway

Ozma of Oz
L Frank Baum

Sound and Bite
Arthur Plotnik

First Hand (Science Poetry)
Linda Bierds

Mere Christianity
C.S. Lewis

Refusing Heaven (Poetry)
Jack Gilbert

Obsidian Butterfly
Laurel K Hamilton

He's Just Not That Into You
Greg Berhendt

What's It All About
Richard De La Chaumiere, PhD

From Barbie to Mortal Kombat
Justine Cassell and Henry Jenkins

Commune: Female Search For Love
bell hooks (again)

Forbidden Faith: Gnostic Legacy
Richard Smoley

The Definitive Book Body Language
Allan and Barbara Pease

Television (6th Ed)
Edited by Horace Newcomb

The Templar Papers
Oddavar Olsen

Carrie
Stephen King

The Talisman
Stephen King and Peter Straub

The End
Lemony Snicket

Elric of Melniborne
Michael Moorcock

The Vanishing Tower
Michael Moorcock

The Revenge of the Rose
Michael Moorcock

Another Day in the Frontal Lobe
Katrina Firlik (Neurosurgeon)

High Fidelity
Nick Hornsby

Encyclopedia of Earth Myths
Richard Leviton (New Age)

Women Writer's: Emily Bronte
Lyn Pykett

Breaking the Spell (Studying Religion)
Daniel C Dennet

Watchmen (Graphic Novel)
Alan Moore

Fortress of the Pearl
Michael Moorcock

Stormbringer
Michael Moorcock

Bowling Alone
Robert Putnam

Klepto
Jenny Pollack

The Russian Intelligence
Michael Moorcock

Inside the Mind of Scott Peterson
Keith Ablow

Tolstoy Lied: A Love Story
Rachel Kadish

Unspeak
Steven Poole

A Mind of Its Own
Cordelia Fine

The Artist's Way
Julia Cameron

Think Like Da Vinci
Michael Glebe

Teach Yourself Jung
Ruth Snowden

Jung's Map of the Soul
Dr. Murray Stein

Emotional Intelligence
Daniel Goleman

Social Intelligence
Daniel Goleman

Denial
Keith Ablow

Projection
Keith Ablow

Psychopath
Keith Ablow

Murder Suicide
Keith Ablow

The Architect
Keith Ablow

Without Mercy
Keith Ablow

Elric at the End of Time
Michael Moorcock

The Unsayable
Annie G Rogers, PhD

The Sociopath Next Door
Martha Stout, Ph.D.

Darkness Visible
William Styron

A Beginners Guide to Reality
Jim Baggott

The God Theory
Bernard Haish

God on Your Own
Joseph Dispenza

Becoming Myself
Willa Shalit

The Things that Matter
Edward Mendelson

Decoding the Universe
Charles Siefe

On Truth
Harry G. Frankfurt

Childhood
Harry Crews

The Sailor on the Seas of Fate
Michael Moorcock

The Bane of the Black Sword
Michael Moorcock

Jung
Deidre Bair

Joe
Larry Brown

A Spy for All Seasons
Duane R Clarridge (Dewy)

Decade of Curious People & Dangerous
Ideas by Chuck Klosterman

Letters of a Portuguese Nun
Myriam Cyr

Stop Dressing Your 6yr Old Like
A Skank by Celia Rivenbark

Reality Check
David L Wiener

Why We Believe What We Believe
Andrew Newberg

The God Gene
Dean Hamer

The Selfish Gene
Richard Dawkins

People of the Lie
M Scott Peck

How To Cope With Depression
DePaulo and Ablow

Out of the Woods
Hauser, Allen and Golden

The Insanity of Normality
Arno Grun

The Divided Self
R.D. Laing

The Happiest Toddler on the Block
Harvey Karp

The Happiest Baby on the Block
Harvey Karp

Beauty
Robin McKinley

Paradox of Oz
Edward Einhorn

Bridge to Terabithia
Katherine Patterson

Any Woman's Blues (Again)
Erica Jong

Fear of Flying (Again)
Erica Jong

Gay in LA
Lillian Fader and Stuart Timmons

Pornified
Pamela Paul

The Science of Desire
Dean Hamer and Peter Copeland

Reading Like A Writer
Francine Prose

Touch Magic
Jane Yolen

From Beast to Blonde
Marina Warner

Lolita (Again)
Vladimir Nabokov

Belinda (Again)
Anne Rice

Night Magic (Again)
Charlotte Vale Allen

Normal Girl (Again)
Molly Jong-Fast

A Brief History of Time
Stephen Hawking

A Theory of Everything
Stephen Hawking

How I Write
Janet Evanovich

Writing Tools
Roy Peter Clark

A Writer's Coach
Jack A Hart

The Verbally Abusive Man
Patricia Evans

Fame Junkies
Jake Halpern

The End of the Affair
Graham Greene (Again)

The House of Incest
Anais Nin (Again)

Zen and the Art of Motorcycle Maintenance
Robert Pirsig

How To See Yourself
Dalai Lama

Bitchfest
Bitch Magazine

This Is Not Chick Lit
Ed Elizabeth Merrick

The Marriage of Sex and Spirit
Editor Geralyn Genreau MFT

The Lost Civilization of Lemuria
Frank Joseph

The Book That Changed My Life
Ed, Coady & Johannessen

20 Essay by 20 Something Writers
Edited by Kellogg and Quint

A Catalogue of Angels
Vinita Hampton Wright

Smashed
Koren Zailckas

Drinking: A Love Story
Caroline Knapp

Somewhere In Time
Richard Matheson

A Girl Named Zippy
Haven Kimmel

Kiss (Again)
Katherine Harrison

Denial (Again)
Keith Ablow

Compulsion (Again)
Keith Ablow

Pissed Off: Women and Anger
Spike Gillespie

Fight Like A Girl
Megan Seely

Franny and Zooey
J.D. Salinger

Marie Antoinette: The Journey
Antoine Frazier

Your Second Pregnancy
Katie Tamony

We Don't Live Here Anymore
Andre Dubus

Meditations From A Movable Chair
Andre Dubus

The Pugilist At Rest
Thom Jones

The Simple Art of Murder
Raymond Chandler

Paint It Black
Janet Fitch

White Oleander (Again)
Janet Fitch

A Drinking Life
Pete Hamill

The Magic Years (Steve Martin)
Morris

A Walk in the Woods
Bill Bryson

I'm A Stranger Here Myself
Bill Bryson

In A Sunburned Country
Bill Bryson

The Beatrice Letters
Lemony Snicket

Bare Bones
Kathy Reiches

Death Du Jour
Kathy Reiches

Deadly Voyage
Kathy Reiches

Girlfriend's Guide To Pregnancy
Vikki Levine

Body, Soul, Baby
Tracy W. Gaudet, MD

Lost: Endangered Species
Cathy Hapka

Lost: Secret Identity
Cathy Hapka

Alice's Adventures in Wonderland
Lewis Carroll

When Things Fall Apart
Pema Chodron

The Places That Scare You
Pema Chodron

Monday Mourning
Kathy Reiches

Grave Secrets
Kathy Reiches

Cross Bones
Kathy Reiches

Christ the Lord: Out of Egypt
Anne Rice

Unhooked
Laura Sessions Stepp

Living the Truth
Keith Ablow

Cross Bones
Kathy Reiches

The Jesus Family Tomb
Jacobovici and Pellegrino

Divisadero
Michael Ondaatje

Horseradish
Lemony Snicket

Lust in Translation
Pamela Druckerman

The Da Vinci Code
Dan Brown (Again)

The Curtain
Milan Kundera

Conversations w/ Joyce Carol Oates
Edited by Lee Milazzo

Sorcerer's Stone
JK Rowling (Again)

Chamber of Secrets
JK Rowling (Again)

Prisoner of Azkaban
JK Rowling (Again)

Goblet of Fire
JK Rowling (Again)

Order of the Phoenix
JK Rowling (Again)

Half-Blood Prince
JK Rowling (Again)

Deathly Hallows
JK Rowling

Written On the Body
Jeanette Winterson

The Moon Pool
Abraham Merritt

Mr. Palomar
Italo Calvino

Reading the Gospel of Judas
Elaine Pageles and Karen Liking

The Everything Gnostic Gospels Bk
Meera Lester

Inferno
Dante Alighieri

Purgatory
Dante Alighieri

Paradise
Dante Alighieri

The Gospel of Mary
Karen L. King

Finding Lost
Nikki Stafford

The Secret Magdalene
Ki Longfellow

Wikinomics
Tapscott and Williams

I Thought It Was Just Me
Brene Brown, PhD

Mistakes Were Made But Not By Me
Carol Tavris and Elliott Aronson

Uncovering Alias
Nikki Stafford and Robyn Burnett

The Trouble With Physics
Lee Smolin

Assumed Alias
Edited by Kevin Weismann

Harry Potter and the Bible
Richard Abanes

Looking For God in Harry Potter
John Granger

Authorized Personnel Only
Alias Guide

Beyond Belief
Elaine Pageles

What Have They Done With Jesus?
Ben Witherington III

The Mystical Life of Jesus
Sylvia Brown

Jesus: The Unauthorized Version
Edited by Mian Ridge

The Jesus Papers
Michael Baigent

Holy Blood, Holy Grail
Baigent, Leigh, Lincoln

Gnostic Gospels
Elaine Pageles

The Feminine Face of God
Anderson and Hopkins

Psychic Children
Sylvia Browne

The Dead Sea Scrolls
Geza Vermes

The Hidden Scrolls
Neil Asher Silberman

The Meaning of the Dead Sea Scrolls
Hershel Shanks

The Mysterious Island
Jules Verne

Plum Lovin'
Janet Evanovich

Twelve Sharp (Again)
Janet Evanovich

The Golden Compass
Philip Pullman

Sylvia and Ted
Emma Tennant

The Writer's Idea Book
Jack Heffron

My Thirteenth Winter
Samantha Abeel

Lean Mean Thirteen
Janet Evanovich

100 Years of Solitude
Gabriel Garcia Marquez

The Subtle Knife
Phillip Pullman

The Gaslight Effect
Robin Stern, PhD

Think For Yourself
Steve Hindes

Jesus and the Riddle Dead
Sea Scrolls by Barbara Thiering

Dubliners
James Joyce

Lost Horizon
James Hilton

Bones to Ashes
Kathy Reiches

Buddha is as Buddha Does
Lama Surya Dass

Atonement
Ian McIwan

Lord or Legend
Boyd and Eddy

God is Not Great
Christopher Hitchens

The Idiots Guide to Verbal Self-Defense
Lillian J Glass PhD

Real Boys
William Pollack PhD

Northanger Abby
Jane Austin

The Psychology of Harry Potter
Editor Neil Mulholland, PhD

The Amber Spyglass
Philip Pullman

Reading List 2008

Judas and Jesus: Two Faces of a Single Revelation Jean-Ives Leloup	The Two Marys Sylvia Browne
Finding Lost Season 3 Nikki Stafford	Secret Societies Sylvia Browne
Born Standing Up Steve Martin	Thus Spoke Zarathustra Friedrich Nietzsche
Spacebread (Again) Steve Senn	Basic Writings of Nietzsche Friedrich Nietzsche
Under The Jaguar Sun Italo Calvino	Criminals Margot Lively
The Baron in the Trees Italo Calvino	The Untouched Key Alice Miller
Notes from the Underbelly Risa Green	The Body Never Lies Alice Miller
Tales from the Crib Risa Green	Breaking Down Wall Silence Alice Miller
Sage-ing while Age-ing Shirley McLaine	Inside Inside James Lipton
Indiana Jones and the Philosopher's Stone Max McCoy	Freethinkers Susan Jacoby
Indiana Jones and the Dinosaur Eggs Max McCoy	The Ruby and The Smoke Philip Pullman
Indiana Jones and the Secret of the Sphinx Max McCoy	Science of His Dark Materials by Mary Gribbin
Indiana Jones and the Hollow Earth Max McCoy	The Magical World of Narnia David Colbert
The Crystal Skull Rob McGregor	The Invention of Morel Casares
Jesus after the Crucifixion Graham Simmans	Valis Philip K Dick

The Queen Jade
Yata Maya Murray

Off The Map
Derrick Nelson

Plum Lucky
Janet Evanovich

Common Sense
Thomas Paine

Age of Reason
Thomas Paine

Age of Unreason
Susan Jacoby

Prince Caspian
CS Lewis (Again)

The Thong Also Rises
Editor Jennifer J Leo

The Third Jesus
Deepak Chopra

Christ the Lord: The Road to Cana
Anne Rice

The Sense of Reality
Isaiah Berlin

Loud as a Whisper
Joel Schwan

Learning Disabilities A-Z
Corrine Smith and Lisa Strick

Diary of a Mad Mom-To-Be
Laura Wolf (Again)

Sober and Staying that Way
Susan Powers

Cleopatra 7.2
Elizabeth Ann Scarborough

Slaughterhouse-Five
Kurt Vonnegut

Breakfast of Champions
Kurt Vonnegut

Cat's Cradle
Kurt Vonnegut

Timequake
Kurt Vonnegut

Hocus Pocus
Kurt Vonnegut

The Truth Heals
Dr. Debora King

Wicked
Gregory McGuire

Ruby Fruit Jungle
Rita Mae Brown

Dress Your Family
David Sedaris

Supernanny
Jo Frost

Losing It
Valerie Bertinelli

Lost and Philosophy
Ed Sharron M Kaye

Chasing Vermeer
Blue Balliet

Girl with a Pearl Earring
Tracey Chevalier

Lost Signs of Life
Frank Thompson

Living Lost
Joley Wood

Climate Confusion
Roy Spencer

Betrayal of Science and Reason
Paul and Anne Ehlrich

The Dawkins Delusion
Alistair and Joanna McGrath

Indiana Jones and the Kingdom of the
Crystal Skull by James Rollins

A Path with Heart
Jack Kornfield (Again)

The House on Fortune Street
Margot Lively

Temples on the Other Side
Sylvia Brown

Skywalking (Again)
Dale Pollack

Mythmaker (Again)
John Baxter

The Oath
John LesCourt

Dark Horse
Tami Hoag

Valhalla Rising
Clive Cusseler

Atlantis Found
Clive Cusseler

The Sheltering Sky
Paul Bowles

The Shape of Things to Come
H G Wells

Lost's Buried Treasures
Lynnette Porter

What Can Be Found In Lost
Ankerberg and Burroughs

Mistral's Kiss
Laurell K Hamilton

A Lick of Frost
Laurell K Hamilton

Getting Lost
Orson Scott Card

Domes of Fire
David Eddings

The Science of Dune
Kevin R Graizer

The Maker of Dune
Edited by Tim O'Reilly

The Illuminatus Trilogy
Shea and Wilson

Loose Girl: A Memoir
Kerry Cohen

Sweet Ruin
Cathi Hanauer

The Atlas of Atlantis & other
Lost Civilizations by Levy

The Rise and Fall of Atlantis
J S Gordon

Atlantis: Ancient Legacy
John Michael Greer

Captain Gault
William Hope Hodges

Trent's Last Case
E C Bentley

Fearless Fourteen
Janet Evanovich

Heroes: Saving Charlie
Aury Wallington

Saving the World: A Guide
To Heroes: Porter and Lavery

Fire in the Mind: Science, Faith
George Johnson

Two-Dollar Bill
Stuart Woods

Dirty Work
Stuart Woods

Night Time is my Time
Mary Higgins Clark

No Place Like Home
Mary Higgins Clark

The Eleventh Hour
Catherine Coulter

It's Up To You
Dzigar Kongtrul

Grassroots Zen
Steger and Besserman

Confessions of a Pagan Nun
Kate Horst

Against Happiness
Eric G Wilson

It's A Break Up Because
It's Broken by Berhendt

The Greatest Generation
Tom Brokaw

Red Man's Religion
Ruth M Underhill

Caravan of Dreams
Idra Sidra

The Road To Oz (Again)
L Frank Baum

The Secret Vampire
L.J. Smith

Top Secret
Robert Price

True Enough
Farhad Manjoo

Legends of Literature
Phillip Sexton Price

Book Smart
Jane Mallison

Reading Group Selections
2009

Fahrenheit 451
Ray Bradbury

Twilight
Stephanie Meyer

The Discoveries of America
Harold Faber

The Fiction Class
Susan Breen

Swallowed By Darkness
Lauren K Hamilton

Real Education
Charles Murray

Smart Kids, Bad Schools
Brian Crosby

In Defense of Food
Michael Pollen

The Omnivores Dilemma
Michael Pollen

Reading List 2009

Audition
Barbara Walters

Catch-22
Joseph Heller

The Spiral Staircase
Karen Armstrong

Jane Eyre (Again)
Charlotte Bronte

Mirroring People
Marco Icoboni

Anne Sexton: A Biography
Diane Middlebrook

Once Were Warriors
Alan Duff

Plum Spooky
Janet Evanovich

Best American
Poetry 2008

Wizard's First Rule
Terry Goodkind

Stone Tears
Terry Goodkind

Blood of the Fold
Terry Goodkind

Soul of the Fire
Terry Goodkind

Pillars of Creation
Terry Goodkind

Naked Empire
Terry Goodkind

Unstuck
James Gordon

How Not To Die
Dr.G

Love and other Natural Disasters
Holly Shumas

Things I've Been Silent About
Azar Nafisi

The Secret History of Dreaming
Robert Moss

Conscious Love: Insights
Richard Smoley

Little Children
Tom Perrotta

Nearer the Moon
Anais Nin

Two Rivers Close To A Dream
Joel Schwan and Lindsay Hughes

Radiant Darkness
Emily Whitman

Pizza: A Global History
Carol Helstosky

The Kosher Sutra
Shmuley Boteach

My Little Red Book
Rachel Kauder Nalebuff,

Live through This
Debra Gwartney

Phantom
Terry Goodkind

Temple of the Winds
Terry Goodkind

A Game of Thrones
George RR Martin

A Clash of Kings
George RR Martin

A Feast for Crows
George RR Martin

A Storm of Swords
George RR Martin

Heart Shaped Box
Joe Hill

The Gnostics
Andrew Philip Smith

Emotional Bullshit
Carl Alasko

God without Religion
Sankara Saranam

Called Out Of Darkness
Anne Rice

Break No Bones
Kathy Riches

Dhampir
Barb and JC Hendee

Child of a Dead God
Barb and JC Hendee

Shade and Shadow
Barb and JC Hendee

Her Only Desire
Galen Foley

Chainfire
Terry Goodkind

Confessor
Terry Goodkind

Embracing the Wide Sky
Daniel Tammet

Counterknowledge
Damian Thompson

Born on a Blue Day
Daniel Tammet

Missionary No More
Zane, Editor (Erotica)

Why Him? Why Her?
Helen Fisher

Short History of Nearly Everything
Bill Bryson

The Kingdom of Infinite Space
Raymond Tallis

The Elfish Gene
Mark Barrowcliff

Possession
A.S. Byatt

Who's Been Sleeping in Your Head?
Brett Kahr

Book (Again)
Whoopie Goldberg

Jim Harrison (Twayne Series)
Edward C Reilly

The Last Templar
Raymond Khoury

On Desire
William B Irvine

The Secret Life of Bees
Sue Monk Kidd (Again)

Granted (Poetry)
Mary Szybist

Collected Works
Flannery O'Connor

A Separate Reality
Carlos Castaneda

The Writings of Pierre Teilhard
De Chardin Ed. by Ursula King

Spirit of Fire (Bio of Teilhard)
Ursula King

The Jesuit and the Skull
Amir De Aczel (Teilhard)

A Prairie Tale (Autobiography)
Melissa Gilbert

The Dependent Gene
David S Moore

Strange Candy
Laurell K Hamilton

A Woman Speaks
Anais Nin (Again)

Novel of the Future
Anais Nin (Again)

Diary Volume 5
Anais Nin (Again)

Diary Volume 6
Anais Nin (Again)

Loud as a Whisper
Joel Schwan (Again)

The Brother of Jesus
Shanks and Witherington

The Little Prince (Again)
Antoine de Saint-Exupery

Asking For It (Erotica)
Tunstall, Wylde and Adams

Emotional Freedom
Judith Orloff

Prey
Michael Crichton

O Pioneers
Willa Cather

The Tale of Genji
Muraskai Shikibu

Diary Volume 7
Anais Nin (Again)

A Journal of Incest
Anais Nin (Again)

The Everything Guide to Edgar
Allen Poe by Shelly Bloomfield

The Survivor's Club
Ben Sherwood

Anais Nin: A Biography
Deidre Bair (Again)

Stuck
Anneli Rufus

On Writing (Again)
Henry Miller

The Books of My Life
Henry Miller (Again)

The Smile at the Foot of the Ladder
Henry Miller

Cat and the Wizard
J Paulette Forshey

Fulfilling Promise
Penelope Jones

What Women Want
Erica Jong (Again)

Dragon Reborn
Robert Jordan

The Sedona Method
Hale Dwoskin

Different Loving
Brame, Brame and Jacobs

Bonk
Mary Roach

Are You There Vodka? It's me Chelsea.
Chelsea Handler

Flash Forward
Robert J Sawyer

The Struggle
LJ Smith (Again)

The Fury
LJ Smith (Again)

206 Bones
Kathy Reiches

Perfume
Patrick Suskind

Sin and Syntax
Constance Hale

The Law of Nines
Terry Goodkind

The Lord of the Rings & Philosophy
Ed Bassham and Bronson

The Survivors of the Chancellor
Jules Verne

It's Not Necessarily the Truth
Jamie Pressly

Star Wars and Philosophy
Edited by Decker and Eberl

Psychic Healing
Sylvia Brown

Finding Oz
Evan I Schwartz

Fooling with Words
Bill Moyers

The Emerald City of Oz
L Frank Baum (Again)

Secrets of the Yellow Brick Road
Jesse Stewart

The Black Swan
Nassim Nicolas Taleb

The Healing of Emotion
Chris Griscom

Feminine Fusion
Chris Griscom

The Four Feathers
A.E.W. Mason

How To Hug A Porcupine
Dr Debbie Ellis

The God Particle
Leon Lederman

Strange Attractors: Chaos
Butz, Chamberlain and McCown

Fooled by Randomness
Nassim Taleb

Dark Nights of the Soul
Thomas Moore (Again)

There and Back Again
Sean Astin

Archetypes and Strange Attractors
John R Van Eenwyk

The Art and Craft of the Short Story
Rick DeMarinis

The Midnight Disease
Alice Weaver Flaherty

Open To Desire
Mark Epstein, MD

Tweak
Nic Sneff

The Pregnant Virgin
Marion Woodman

Dancing in the Flames
Marion Woodman & Elinor Dickson

Nurture Shock
Po Bronson & Ashley Merryman

Bright-Sided
Barbara Ehenreich

Zen Reflections
James H Austin, MD

Suck It Up
Brian Meehl

True Mom Confessions
Romi Lassally

The Discovery of Global Warming
Spencer R Weart

God, the Universe and Where I Fit In
Laurie Ann Levin

Six Word Memoirs on Love and
Heartbreak: Edited Smith Magazine

The Essence of Chaos
Edward Lorenz

Anais Nin & Remaking of the Self
Diane Richard-Allerdyce (Again)

Anais Nin Narratives
Anne T Salvatore (Again)

Anais Nin an Introduction
Franklin and Schneider (Again)

Anais Nin
Nancy Scholar (Again)

Behind The Bell
Dustin Diamond

Why Women Have Sex
Meston and Bess

The Plumed Serpent
DH Lawrence

The Lost Girl
DH Lawrence

The Fox, The Captain, Ladybird
DH Lawrence

Contemplative Science
B Alan Wallace

Star Trek (2009)
Alan Dean Foster

The Ethical Slut (2nd Ed 2009)
Dossie Easton and Janet W Hardy

Emotions Revealed
Paul Ekman

Delete: The Virtue of Forgetting
Viktor Mayer-Shonberger

The Time of My Life
Patrick Swayze and Lisa Niemi

Lit
Mary Karr

Leaving My Father's House
Marion Woodman

Dragonsdawn
Anne McCaffery

The White Queen
Philippa Gregory

The Virgin's Lover
Philippa Gregory

The Other Boleyn Girl
Philippa Gregory

The Other Queen
Philippa Gregory

The Boleyn Inheritance
Philippa Gregory

Telling Lies
Paul Ekman

Lying and Deception in Everyday Life
Ed Lewis and Saarni

The Life and Times of the
Thunderbolt Kid by Bill Bryson

Beowulf on the Beach
Jack Murnigha

The 2012 Story
John Major Jenkins

The Tao of Chaos
Katya Walter

Quantum Gods
Victor J Stenger

Super Freakonomics
Levit and Dubner

The Writer's I Ching

The Gutenberg Galaxy
Marshall McLuhan

Reading Lost
Ed Roberta Pearson

The Third Policeman
Flan O'Brian

The Boy in the Bush
D.H. Lawrence

Finding Lost Season 4
Nikki Stafford

Lost's Buried Treasures Ed 3
Lynnette Porter

The Myth of Lost
Marc Oromaner

Lost Ate My Life
Lachonis and Johnston

The Wisdom of Your Dreams
Jeremy Taylor

Finding Lost Season 5
Nikki Stafford

Haroun & The Sea of Stories
Salman Rushdie

The Essential Kierkegaard
Edited by Hong

Glory Road
Robert A Heinlein

Living Lost
J Wood (Again)

HP and the Deathly Hallows
JK Rowling (Again)

Out of the Silent Planet
CS Lewis

Beyond the Gutenberg Galaxy
Eugene F Provenzo Jr.

The Joy of Text
Kristina Gish

People Are Unappealing
Sara Barron

The Kid
Dan Savage

The Fifth Agreement
Don Miguel Ruiz

The Romance of Libraries
Ed by Lefebvre and Gorman

Wildly Romantic
Catherine M Andronik

Connected
Christakis and Fowler

Revolutionary Road
Richard Yates

Point Omega
Don DeLillo

The Humbling
Philip Roth

The Anthologist
Nicholas Baker

What French Women Know
Debra Olivier

Curious
Todd Kashdan, PhD

Face it and Fix it
Ken Seely

Finding It
Valerie Bertinelli

Perelandra
CS Lewis

That Hideous Strength
CS Lewis

The Way into Narnia
Peter J Schakel

A Kiss of Shadows
Laurell K Hamilton (Again)

Stardust
Neil Gaimen

Coraline
Neil Gaimen

Divine Misdemeanors
Laurell K Hamilton

Living with the Devil
Stephen Batchelor

The Awakening of the West
Stephen Batchelor

Beneath the Mask of
Holiness by Mark Shaw

Confessions of a Buddhist
Atheist by Stephen Batchelor

A Caress of Twilight
Laurell K Hamilton (Again)

Seduced by Moonlight
Laurell J Hamilton (Again)

A Stroke of Midnight
Laurell K Hamilton (Again)

A Lick of Frost
Laurell K Hamilton (Again)

The Chosen
Chaim Potak

Love is a Four Letter Word
Ed Michael Taekens

The Art of Happiness in a Troubled World
Dalai Lama and Howard Cutler

A History of Egypt
Jason Thompson

The Time Traveler's Wife
Audrey Niffenegger

The Lost Symbol
Dan Brown

Searching For Suzi
Nancy Stohlman

The Silent Sea
Clive Cussler

Vampire Diaries: Dark Reunion
LJ Smith (Again)

Vampire Diaries: Nightfall
LJ Smith

Vampire Diaries: Shadow Souls
LJ Smith

Raising Happiness
Christine Carter

Crash Course in Love
Steve Ward and JoAnn Ward

No Death, No Fear
Thich Nhat Hanh

Lovely Bones
Alice Sebold

Lucky
Alice Sebold

I am an Emotional Creature
Eve Ensler

The Lovers
Kate Hawks

What I Thought I Knew
Alice Eve Cohen

The Immortal Realm
Frewin Jones

What Katy Read
Foster & Simons

The Return: Nightfall
Vampire Diaries by LJ Smith

Haunted Heart (S King)
Lisa Rogak

20th Century Ghost Stories
Joe Hill

Notes from the Underground
Dostoyevsky

The End of Eternity
Isaac Asimov

Masks of the Universe
Edward Harrison

Planets
Dava Sobel

Parallel Worlds
Michio Kaku

Adam, Eve & the Serpent
Elaine Pagles

Harry Potter & Philosophy
Ed Baggett and Klein

Laughter in the Dark
Vladimir Nabokov

Pale Fire
Vladimir Nabokov

The Forty Rules of Love
Elif Shafa

Alice in Wonderland and Philosophy
Ed Richard Brian Davis

101 Theory Drive
Terry McDermott

Convergence Culture
Henry Jenkins

The Secret Life of the Grown-Up Brain
Barbara Strauch

The Law of the Jungle
John Otis

Instinctive Parenting
Ada Calhoun

Little House on the Prairie
Laura Ingles Wilder

Little Town on the Prairie
Laura Ingles Wilder

The Reincarnationist
MJ Rose

The Memoirist
MJ Rose

The Hypnotist
MJ Rose

How To Publish and Promote On Line
MJ Rose and Angela Adair-Hoy

Lip Service
MJ Rose

Writer's Market 2010
Writer's Guide To Getting Published

Good without God
Greg M Epstein

Reading and the Brain
Stanislaus Dehaene

The Truth About Psychics
Sylvia Browne

Consequential Strangers
M Blau and Karen Fingerman

Committed
Elizabeth Gilbert

From Eternity to Here
Sean Carroll

Born For Love
Perry and Maia Szalavitz

Spiritual Partners
Gary Zukav

Angel Time
Anne Rice

How Uncover Past Lives
Ted Andrews

Coming Back
Raymond Moody

Children's Past Lives
Carol Bowman

Life Before Life
Jim B Tucker

Psychic: My Life Two Worlds
Sylvia Browne

The Bastard of Istanbul
Elif Shafak

Her Fearful Symmetry
Audrey Niffenegger

Blues Lessons
Robert Helena

How Do You Tuck In A Superhero
Rachel Balducci

The Queen's Fool
Philippa Gregory

The Red Queen
Philippa Gregory

Angelina
Andrew Norton

Between a Heart and a Rock Place
Pat Benatar

Percy Jackson Lightening Thief
Rick Riordan

Percy Jackson Sea Monster
Rick Riordan

Percy Jackson Titans Curse
Rick Riordan

Percy Jackson Battle of the Labyrinth
Rick Riordan

The Girl with The Dragon Tattoo
Stieg Larsson

The Girl Who Kicked a Hornet's Nest
Stieg Larson

Taking the Leap
Pema Chodron

Practicing Peace in Times of War
Pema Chodron

Always Maintain A Joyful Mind
Pema Chodron

The Wisdom of No Escape
Pema Chodron

Comfortable With Uncertainty
Pema Chodron

The Twenty-Four Hour Mind
Rosalind D Cartwright

Sizzling Sixteen
Janet Evanovich

Eat, Pray, Love,
Elizabeth Gilbert

Medicine in Translation
Dr. Danielle Offri

Reality: A Manifesto
David Shields

Overclocked: Short Stories
Cory Doctorow

That Perfect Someone
Johanna Lindsay

Love & Other Impossible Pursuits
Ayelet Walden

Bad Mother
Ayelet Walden

The Girl Who Played with Fire
Stieg Larsson

The Murder of King Tut
James Patterson

Imperfect Birds
Anne Lamott

Inseparables
Emma Donoghue

Gentle Rogue
Johanna Lindsey

Spider Bones
Kathy Reiches

The Pearl of China
Achee Min

Start Where You Are
Pema Chodron

Healing Through The Dark Emotions
Marian Greenspan

The Purpose-Guided Universe
Bernard Haisch

Talking To Girls About Duran Duran
Rob Sheffield

Love is a Mix Tape
Rob Sheffield

Long For This Life
Jonathan Wiener

The Shinning Ones
Philip Gardiner and Gary Osborn

A Tear At The Edge of Creation
Marcelo Geliser

Rewired
Larry D Rosen, PhD

The Genius In All of Us
David Shenk

The Destructors (Short Story)
Graham Greene

The Lost Encyclopedia
Paul Terry and Tara Bennet

The Initiation
LJ Smith

The Captive
LJ Smith

Witches Sister
Phyllis Reynolds Naylor

A Dozen on Denver
Rocky Mountain News

Rewriting
Christian Moraru

Decoding Reality
Vlatko Vedral

Dead in the Family
Charlaine Harris

Dead and Gone
Charlaine Harris

Bite Me
Nikki Stafford

Xena and Gabrielle
Nikki Stafford

Finding Lost Season 6
Nikki Stafford

The Grand Design
Stephen Hawking

Delusions of Gender
Cordelia Fine

Witch Water
Phyllis Reynolds Naylor

Witch Herself
Phyllis Reynolds Naylor

By Nightfall
Michael Cunningham

The Nearest Exit
Olen Steinhauer

The Tourist
Olen Steinhauer

The 2012 Codex
Gary Jennings

Unhinged: Trouble With Psychiatry
Daniel J Carlat, MD

Oprah: A Biography
Kitty Kelley

The Good Man Jesus and
The Scoundrel Christ
Phillip Pullman

Reading List 2011

Shakespeare: The World as Stage
Bill Bryson

Wicked Appetite
Janet Evanovich

Out of Time (Kindle)
Monique Martin

The Maiden King
Robert Bly & Marion Woodman

Hard Sell
Jamie Reidy

Luka and the Fire of Life
Salman Rushdie

Lips Unsealed: A Memoir
Belinda Carlisle

Liespotting
Pamela A Meyer

At Home
Bill Bryson

Louisa May Alcott
Susan Cheever

The Poisoner's Handbook
Deborah Blum

Spiritual Teachings of the Avatar
Jeffery Armstrong

The 7 Wonders
Keith Ablow & Glen Beck

With Love and Laughter John Ritter
Amy Yasbeck

Off To The Side
Jim Harrison

The English Patient
Michael Ondaatje (Again)

Misery
Stephen King

The Other Brain
R Douglas Fields, PhD

Heaven
Lisa Miller

Book of Dreams
Sylvia Browne

You Can Get to Here From
Shirley MacLaine (Again)

Horns
Joe Hill

The Postcard Killers
James Patterson

The Two Mary's
Sylvia Browne (Again)

The Wide Window
Lemony Snicket (Again)

The Miserable Mill
Lemony Snicket (Again)

The Austere Academy
Lemony Snicket (Again)

The Ersatz Elevator
Lemony Snicket (Again)

The Vile Village (Again)
Lemony Snicket

The Hostile Hospital
Lemony Snicket (Again)

The Year of Magical Thinking
Joan Didion

Negotiating With The Dead
Margaret Atwood

The Truth About Grief
Ruth Davis Konigsberg

How Music Works
John Powell

Up In The Air
Walter Kirn

The Lady and the Unicorn
Tracy Chevalier

Poser: My Life in 23 Yoga Poses
Claire Dederer

Prozac Nation (Again)
Elizabeth Wurtzle

An Unquiet Mind (Again)
Kay Redfield Jamison

Imzadi (Again)
Peter David

Bad Behavior
Mary Gaitskill

Literary Lost
Sarah Clarke Stuart

Love and Love Sickness
John Money

Is It Just Me Or Is It Nuts Out There?
Whoppi Goldberg

The Truth Will Set You Free
Alice Miller

Paths of Life
Alice Miller

The Carnivorous Carnival
Lemony Snicket (Again)

Naked Edge
Pamela Clare (Boulder)

Amazon Ink
Lori Devoti

Kiss At Your Own Risk
Stephanie Rowe

Dominic: King of the Satyrs
Elizabeth Amber

The Pirate Hunter
Jennifer Ashley

The Vampire Shrink
Lynda Hilburn (Boulder)

The Shallows
Nicholas Carr (Colorado)

Deadly Lies
Cynthia Eden

Past Lives, Future Healing
Sylvia Browne

Don't Blink
James Patterson

The Lover's Dictionary
David Levithan

Prophecy
Sylvia Browne

Murder in Vein
Sue Ann Jaffaria

The Return: Midnight
LJ Smith (Vampire Diaries)

Q-In-Law (Again)
Peter David

Prisoners of Childhood: Drama of
The Gifted Child by Alice Miller

Banished Knowledge
Alice Miller

Be Love Know
Ram Dass

Be Here Now, Remember
Ram Dass

My Spiritual Journey
Dalai Lama

What We Ache For
Oriah Mountain Dreamer

The Wise Heart
Jack Kornfield

Mystical Traveler
Sylvia Browne

The Fabric of the Universe
Brian Greene

A Hidden Reality
Brian Greene

The Twelve Wild Swans
Starhawk & Hilary Valentine

Webs of Power
Starhawk

The Earth Path
Starhawk

IBD: Self-Management
Sunanda V Kane, MD

You Are Here
Thich Nhat Hanh

Everything Celtic Wisdom
Jennifer Emick

The Empathy Gap
JD Trout

Ecstasy in a New Frequency
Chris Griscom (Again)

Radical Self-Forgiveness
Colin Tipping

The Celtic Way of Seeing
Frank MacEowen

Against the Stream
Noah Levine

Paganism: An Introduction
Joyce and River Higginbotham

Sylvia Plath: A Literary Life
Linda Wagner-Martin

The Art of Losing: Poems on
Grief & Healing Kevin Young

Gnostic Philosophy
Tobias Churton

Vital Lies and Simple Truths
Daniel Goleman

Best American Short Stories
Editor Richard Russo

Blake and Tradition
Kathleen Raine

Sometimes I Act Crazy
Kreisman and Straus

Can Love Last?
Stephen A Mitchell, PhD

A General Theory of Love
Lewis, Amini and Lannon

Intimate Terrorism
Michael Vincent Miller, PhD

Goddess Alive
Michelle Sky

Wicca The Complete Craft
DJ Conway

I Can Read You Like A Book
Gregory Hartley & Maryann Karinch

Unfamiliar Fishes
Sarah Vowell (Kindle)

Defy Gravity
Caroline Myss

The Hidden Brain
Shankar Vedantam

Loneliness
Cacioppo and Patrick

The Liar in Your Life
Robert Feldman

The Journey from Heartbreak
To Connection by Susan Anderson

Assassination Vacation
Sarah Vowell

The Husband and Wives Club
Laurie Abraham

Listening to Prozac
Peter Kramer, MD

The Hungry Season
T Greenwood

Tales from the Grimm Brothers
and Weird Sisters by Velde

A Well-Timed Enchantment
Vivian Vande Velde

Poker Face: Lady Gaga
Maureen Callahan

Dreamgates
Robert Moss

Me
Ricky Martin

The Cowboy and the Vampire
Clark Hayes and Kathleen McFall

Active Dreaming
Robert Moss

The Source of All Things
Tracy Ross (Boulder)

The Mythic Imagination
Stephen Larson, PhD

The Cloudy Patriot
Sarah Vowell

Take the Cannoli
Sarah Vowell

The Wordy Shipmates
Sarah Vowell

Shaman, Sage, Healer
Albert Villoldo, PhD

Four Winds
Alberto Villoldo, PhD

Courageous Dreaming
Alberto Villoldo, PhD

The Science of the Dogon
Laid Scranton

The Haitian Vodou Handbook
Kenaz Filan (Coquille De Mer)

Cursing, Inc and Other Stories
Vivian Vande Velde

Dragon's Bait
Vivian Vande Velde

Companion of the Night
Vivian Vande Velde

Never Trust A Dead Man
Vivian Vande Velde

A Concise Chinese-English Dictionary
For Lovers by Xiaolu Guo

Secrets To Happiness
Sarah Dunn

The Big Love
Sarah Dunn

In Fidelity
MJ Rose

The Halo Effect
MJ Rose

Sheet Music
MJ Rose

The Constant Princess
Philippa Gregory

Shameless
Karen Robards

Ruthless Game
Christine Feehan

Street Game
Christine Feehan

Work of Heart
Cindy Myers (Boulder)

Yoga, Power and Spirit
Alberto Villoldo

Secret Mysteries of the World
Sylvia Browne

Vampires Today
Joseph Laycock

She Walks With Men
Ann Beatie

Dark Challenge
Christine Feehan

Dark Secret
Christine Feehan

Dark Demon
Christine Feehan

Dark Slayer
Christine Feehan

Dark Peril
Christine Feehan

Fever
Christine Feehan

Savage Nature
Christine Feehan

Dark Dreamers
Christine Feehan

Predatory Game
Christine Feehan

Deadly Game
Christine Feehan

Seeking the Sacred
Stephanie Dowrick

The City of Ember
Jeanne DuPrau

Inkheart
Cordelia Funke

Island of the Sun
Albert Villoldo

Finder's Keepers
Craig Childs

The World of Shamanism
Roger Walsh, MD and PhD

My Sister Madonna
Christopher Ciccone

Like an Icon (Madonna)
Lucy O'Brian

Mariah Carey
Marc Shapiro

Full Frontal Feminism
Jessica Valenti

Stefan's Diary: Origins
LJ Smith

Stefan's Diaries: Bloodlust
LJ Smith
Kreisberg

Totally Charmed (TV)
Jennifer Cruise, Ed

Sugar in my Bowl
Editor Erica Jong

True You
Janet Jackson

The Horse and His Boy
CS Lewis (Again)

The Three Only Things
Robert Moss

The Gift Giver
Jennifer Hawkins

Jaded
Karin Tabke

Jailbait Zombie
Mario Acevedo (Denver)

X-Rate Blood Suckers
Mario Acevedo (Denver)

The Undead Kama Sutra
Mario Acevedo (Denver)

Nymphos of the Rocky Flat
Mario Acevedo (Denver)

Werewolf Smackdown
Mario Acevedo (Denver)

Pillars of Creation
Ken Follett

Critical Companion To Ken Follett
Richard C Turner (1996)

Lost Knowledge of the Ancients
Graham Hancock Reader, Ed

Underworld: Mysterious Origins
Graham Hancock

A Helluva High Note
Kara Dioguardi

Still Missing
Chevy Stevens

A Dance of Dragons
George RR Martin

Beastly
Alex Flinn

Breathing Underwater
Alex Flinn

I'm Not Dead, I'm Different
Hollister Rand

There's A Dead Person Following My
Sister Around Vivian Van Velde

You Can't Drink All Day If You Don't
Start in The Morning by Celia Rivenbark

Hypatia of Alexandria
Michael A B Deakin

A Planet of Viruses
Carl Zimmer

The Vampire and the Virgin
Kerrelyn Sparks

Forbidden Night with a Vampire
Kerrelyn Sparks

Vampire Mine
Kerrelyn Sparks

Be Still My Vampire Heart
Kerrelyn Sparks

Eat, Prey, Love
Kerrelyn Sparks

Secret Life of a Vampire
Kerrelyn Sparks

All I Want For Christmas Is A Vampire
Kerrelyn Sparks

The Sexiest Vampire
Kerrelyn Sparks

Dark Predator
Christine Feehan

Derby Girl
Shauna Cross

Bird By Bird
Anne Lamott

Fade To Black
Alexi Flinn

A Kiss in Time
Alex Flinn

Cloaked
Alex Flinn

Nothing To Lose
Alex Flinn

Breaking Point
Alex Flinn

The Ghost
Robert Harris

Fair Game: Life As A Spy
Valerie Plame Wilson

The Dark Fields
Alan Glynn

The Quantum Thief
Hannu Rajaniemi

Smokin' Seventeen
Janet Evanovich

Flash and Bones
Kathy Reichs

The Undead Next Door
Kerrelyn Spark

Soulless (Steampunk)
Gail Carriger

Mainspring (Steampunk)
Jay Lake

Steampunk Trilogy
Paul Di Filippo

The Manual of Detection
Jedediah Berry (Steampunk)

Fingerprints of The Gods
Graham Hancock

Mirror of Heaven
Graham Hancock

Denial and Deception (CIA)
Melissa Boyle Mahle

Hubris (CIA)
Isikoff and Corn

On the Brink (CIA)
Tyler Drumheller

Colorado Springs
Elizabeth Wallace (Arcadia)

Colorado's Castles
Anne Westerberg

Aurora (Arcadia)
Sherah J Collins

Denver's Sixteenth Street
Mark A Barnhouse (Arcadia)

Denver's Early Architecture
James Bretz (Arcadia)

Denver's Capitol Hill Neighborhood
Amy B Zimmer (Arcadia)

Denver's City Park and Whittier Neighborhoods
Shawn M Snow (Arcadia)

University Park and South Denver
Edited by Nick Gevers (Arcadia)

Denver's Park Hill Neighborhood
Rebecca C Dorward (Arcadia)

It Happened In Colorado
James A Crutchfield

Boneshaker (Steampunk)
Cherie Priest

Clockwork Heart
Dru Pagliassotti (Steampunk)

The Glass Book of the Dream Eaters
Gordon Dahlquist, Vol. 1

The Glass Book of the Dream Eaters
Gordon Dahlquist, Vol. 2

The Difference Engine (Steampunk)
William Gibson and Bruce Sterling

Pavane (Steampunk)
Keith Roberts

Zeppelins West (Steampunk)
Joe R Lansdale

The Hunchback Assignments
Arthur Slade (Steampunk)

Dreadnought (Steampunk)
Cherie Priest

Not Flesh Nor Feathers
Cherie Priest

Four and Twenty Blackbirds
Cherie Priest

Ganymede (Steampunk)
Cherie Priest

Hellbent (Vampire)
Cherie Priest

Bloodshot (Vampire)
Cherie Priest

Changeless (Steampunk)
Gail Carriger

Hidden History of Denver
Elizabeth Victoria Wallace

Just A Geek
Wil Wheaton

The Lincoln Lawyer
Michael Connelly

The Snowman
Jo Nesbo

Snow Flower and the Secret Fan
Lisa See

Psychic Intelligence
Terry and Lynda Jamison

Truly, Madly, Deadly
Becca Wilcott (True Blood)

Stefan's Diaries: The Craving
LJ Smith (Vampire)

Love You to Death: Season 2
Crissy Calhoun (Vampire Diaries)

The Hunters: Phantom
LJ Smith (Vampire Diaries)

The Fury and Dark Reunion
LJ Smith (Vampire Diaries)

The Rest Falls Away
Coleen Gleason (Vampire)

Rises The Night
Coleen Gleason (Vampire)

Blue Bloods (Vampire)
Melissa De La Cruz

Entwined (Argonauts)
Elizabeth Naughton

Upstairs Girls: Prostitution
Michael Rutter

Blameless (Steampunk)
Gail Carriger

Heartless (Steampunk)
Gail Carriger

The Art of Steampunk
Art Donovan

Extraordinary Engines (Steampunk)
Steve Fisher

Steampunk Anthology
Edited by Ann and Jeff Vandermeer

Steampunk Reloaded
Edited by Ann and Jeff Vandermeer

Dreadful Skin
Cherie Priest

Crystal Rain (Steampunk)
Tobias S Buckell

Leviathan (Steampunk)
Scott Westerfeld

Behemoth (Steampunk)
Scott Westerfeld

Corsets and Clockwork (13 Steampunk
Romances) Editor Trisha Telep

The Girl in the Steel Corset
Kady Cross (Steampunk)

Steampunk: Anthology of Fantastically
Rich and Strange Stories, Ed Link & Grant

1000 Steampunk Creations
Dr. Grymm

The Steampunk Bible
Jeff Vandermeer

Clockwork Angel
Cassandra Clare (Steampunk)

The Queen of Water
Laura Resau

The Lady of the River
Philippa Gregory

Never Knowing
Chevy Stevens

The 4 Percent Universe
Richard Panek

Commerce City (Arcadia)
Debra Bullock

A Quick History of Idaho Springs
Beth Simmons

Silver Saga: Story of Caribou, Colorado
Duane A Smith

Conversations with Joss Whedon
Ed David Laverty

Into The Looking Glass: Fringe
Sarah Clarke Stuart

The Girl Who Circumnavigated Fairyland
In A Ship of Her Own Making
Catherynne M Valente

There Are Things I Want You To Know About
Stieg Larsson and Me
Eva Gabrielsson

Inside the Mind of Casey Anthony
Keith Ablow

Camera Obscura
Lavie Tidhar (Steampunk)

Dead Souls
Nikolai Gogol

The Faerie Ring
Kiki Hamilton

Things I Say With Readings
Ed Graff, Berkensein and Durst

In the Company of Rilke
Stephanie Dowrick

The Creator of Oz
Katherine M Rogers

Oz and Beyond
Michael O'Riley

The Royal Book of Oz
Ruth Plumly Thompson

The Gnome King of Oz
Ruth Plumly Thompson

The Giant Horse of Oz
Ruth Plumly Thompson

Jack The Pumpkinhead of Oz
Ruth Plumly Thompson

Big Bad Wolf
Christine Warren

Bite Me If You Can
Lindsay Sands

The Renegade Hunter
Lindsay Sands

Neon Angel
Cherie Curie

Joan Jett
Todd Oldham

Across the Universe
Beth Revis

Beyond Religion
The Dalia Lama

Early Lakewood
Robert and Kristin Autobee

The Doomsday Vault
Steven Harper

Spirit Bound
Christine Feehan

Explosive Eighteen
Janet Evanovich

Heat Rising
Richard Castle

The Iron Duke
Meljean Brook

Shockoholic
Carrie Fisher

One Click
Richard L Brandt

Miss Peregrine's Home For
Peculiar Children by Riggs

The Graveyard Book
Neil Gaimen

The Omen Machine
Terry Goodkind

The Steal History Shoplifting
Rachel Shteir

Remembering Raquel
Vivian Vande Velde

Wizard's Work
Vivian Vande Velde

Thoughts Without A Thinker
Mark Epstien, MD

The Ripper Vampire Diaries
LJ Smith

The Asylum Vampire Diaries
LJ Smith

Knocking on Heaven's Door
Lisa Randell

Love in a Nutshell
Janet Evanovich

Striptease
Rachel Shteir

Private Parts
Jeff Jarvis

What Would Google Do?
Jeff Jarvis

Connectum
Sebastian Seung

Seizure
Kathy Reiches

True Strength
Kevin Sorbo

The Best American Travel Writing
Sloane Crosley, Ed

Manic: A Memoir
Terri Cheney

The Dark Side of Innocence
Terri Cheney

Madness
Marya Hornabach

The Center Cannot Hold
Elyn R Saks

Skin Game
Caroline Kettlewell

Ash
Malinda Lo

Luna
Julie Ann Peters

Fallen
Thomas Sniegoski

Leviathan
Thomas Sniegoski

Aerie
Thomas Sniegoski

The Reckoning
Thomas Sniegoski

Cinder
Marissa Meyer

Heir Apparent
Vivian Vande Velde

User Friendly
Vivian Vande Velde

Why Be Happy When You
Could Be Normal? Winterson

Go Ask Ogre
Jolene Siana (Again)

Timeless
Gail Carriger

Free Ride
Robert Levine

A Bright Red Scream
Marilee Strong

Cutting
Steve Levenkron

Bodies Under Siege
Armando Favazzo

The Cat's Table
Michael Ondaatje

The Delivery Room
Sylvia Brownrigg

Morality Tale
Sylvia Brownrigg

Getting the Pretty Back
Molly Ringwald

Enchantments
Kathryn Harrison

The Mother Knot
Kathryn Harris

Seeking Rapture
Kathryn Harrison

Harry: A History
Marissa Anelli

Minding the Body
Patricia Foster, Ed

Lighthouse Keeping
Jeanette Winterson

The Powerbook
Jeanette Winterson

The Stone Gods
Jeanette Winterson

The Jesus Discovery
Tabor and Jacobovici

The Hunters: Moonsong
LJ Smith (Vampire Diaries)

Ragnarok
A.S. Byatt

Some Assembly Required
Anne Lamott w/ Sam Lamott

The Jesus Mysteries
Freke and Gandy

Jesus and the Lost Goddess
Freke and Gandy

The Laughing Jesus
Freke and Gandy

Moonwalking with Einstein
Joshua Foer

Man Seeks God
Eric Weiner

Building Better Blueprints
for Girls by Elissa Schappell

Paranormal
Raymond Moody

The Autism Puzzle
Brita Belli

The Prestige
Christopher Priest

Game of Thrones Philosophy
Irwin and Jacoby

Mad Men and Philosophy
William Irwin, Ed

Shamanic Wisdom Keepers
Timothy Freke

From Dead To Worse
Charlene Harris (True Blood)

Clash of Kings (Again)
George RR Martin

A Storm of Swords (Again)
George RR Martin

A Feast For Crows (Again)
George RR Martin

Ophelia
Lisa Klein

Lady Macbeth's Daughter
Lisa Klein

Cate of the Lost Colony
Lisa Klein

Two Girls of Gettysburg
Lisa Klein

Dearly Departed
Lia Habel

The Language Wars
Henry Hitchings

Evelyn, Evelyn (Book 1&2)
Amanda Palmer and Jason Webley

The Girl with the Dragon Tattoo and Philosophy
Edited by Eric Bronson and William Irwin

Inception and Philosophy
Edited by William Irwin

Dreaming the Soul Back Home
Robert Moss

Deadlocked (True Blood)
Charlaine Harris

The Forest of Teeth and Hands
Carrie Ryan

The Dead Tossed Waves
Carrie Ryan

The Dark and Hollow Places
Carrie Ryan

How to Get Into the Top Colleges
Montauk and Kline

A Dance of Dragons (Again)
George RR Martin

A Game of Thrones
George RR Martin (Again)

Malinche
Laura Esqivel

Fifty Shades of Darker
EL James

Fifty Shades of Gray
EL James

Fifty Shades of Free
EL James

Blood and Whiskey
Hays and McFall

The Wolf Gift
Anne Rice

Wicked Business
Janet Evanovich

Fear and Loathing at Rolling
Stone by Hunter S Thompson

She, Myself and I
Whitley Gaitskill

Wanted Undead or Alive
Kerrelynn Sparks

A Crack in the Sky
Mark Peter Hughes

Jake Ransom and the
Skull King's Shadow
James Rollins

Jake Ransom: Howling
Sphinx by James Rollins

Winning Strategies for Getting
Into Graduate School by Mumby

MBA Admissions Strategy
Avi Gordon

How Too Get Into The Top Law
Schools by Montauk

My First Book of Arabic Words
Katy R Kudela

Learn Arabic Fast and Fun Way
Ragy Ibrahim

Guts: Endless Follies, Tiny Triumphs
Kristin Johnston

Ghost Knight
Cornelia Funke

Isis: A Tale of the Supernatural
Douglas Clegg

Revolution 2.0
Wael Gohonim

Destination Mars
Rod Pyle

The Search for Wanderla
Tony Diterlizzi

The Hero for Wanderla
Tony Diterlizzi

Mr. CSI
Anthony E Zuiker

The Girl in the Clockwork Collar
Kady Cross

Bones are Forever
Kathy Reiches

A Certain Slant of Light
Laura Whitcomb

The Judas Strain
James Rollins

Level 26: Dark Origins
Anthony E. Zuiker

Egypt: The Book of Chaos
Nick Drake

Nefertiti: The Book of Dead
Nick Drake

I'm Over That
Shirley McLaine

Traveling w/ Pomegranates
Sue Monk Kidd

Denver Inside and Out
Colorado History #16 2011

What Bleep Do We Know?
Jack Forem and Ellen Erwin

The Physics of the Future
Michio Kaku

ReVamped
Lucienne Diver

The Rope
Nevada Barr

Flash and Bone
Kathy Reiches

Heat Wave
Richard Castle

FBI Girl
Maura Conlon-McIvor

Justine
Marquis De Sade

When Things Fall Apart
Pema Chodron (Again)

The Fetch
Laura Whitcomb

Wolf Brother
Michelle Paver

Stonewolf
Brenda Seabrooke

Zombies Don't Cry
Rusty Fischer

Casual Vacancy
JK Rowling

The Real Crash
Peter Schiff

The Light Inside The Dark
John Tarrant (Zen)

CSI: Double Dealer
Max Allan Collins

Jeneration X
Jen Lancaster

If You Were Here
Jen Lancaster

My Fair Lazy
Jen Lancaster

Bitter is the New Black
Jen Lancaster

Such A Pretty Fat
Jen Lancaster

Hotel
Arthur Hailey

Russia: A 1,000 Chronicle
Martin Sixsmith

What Its Like to Go To War
Karl Marlentes

The Places That Scare Us
Pema Chodron (Again)

The Autism Book
Dr. Sears

Space Chronicles
Neil de Grasse Tyson

Kicking and Dreaming
Ann and Nancy Wilson

The Edge of the Universe
Paul Halpern

Aspergers in Love
Maxine Aston

Angst: Origins of Anxiety
and Depression by Kahn

In the President's Secret
Service by Ronald Kessler

The Secret Service
Phillip Melanson

Heath Ledger
John McShane

Heath Ledger: Dark Star
Brian J Robb

Incarnation
Emma Cornwell

Runaway Girl
Carissa Phelps

Exploring JRR Tolkien's
The Hobbit by Corey Olsen

Friday Society
Adrianne Kress

Sapphire Blue
Kerstin Gier

Under The Sabers
Tanya Biank

Inexplicables
Cherie Priest

The Particle at the End of the Universe
Sean Carroll

Notorious Nineteen
Janet Evanovich

Haunting Violet
Alyandra Harvey

Interview With A Vampire: Claudia's Story
Anne Rice with Ashley Marie Witter

The Fractal Prince
Hannu Rajaniemi

Apocalyptic Planet
Craig Childs

The Mayan Ouroboros
Drunvalo Melchizedek

The True History of Merlin the Magician
Anne Lawrence Mathers

Snow In Summer
Jane Yolen

You Can't Lie To Me
Janine Driver

Mine All Mine
Adam Davies

Click: A Novel in Parts
Various Authors

Best American Short Stories 2012 Ed Tom Perrotta	Sorcerers Stone JK Rowling (To Ana)
Best American Essays 2012 Ed David Brooks	Chamber of Secrets JK Rowling (To Ana)
Both Flesh and Not David Foster Wallace	Prisoner of Azkaban JK Rowling (To Ana)
You Can't Make This Stuff Up Lee Gutkind	Goblet of Fire JK Rowling (To Ana)
Ancient Rome Thomas H Martin	Order of the Phoenix JK Rowling (To Ana)
Spectrums David Blatner	Half Blood Prince JK Rowling (To Ana)
Catching Fire Susan Collins	Deathly Hallows JK Rowling (To Ana)
Mocking Jay Susan Collins	The Event of Literature Terry Eagleton
The Hunger Games and Philosophy Ed William Irwin	Medusa's Gaze & Vampire Bite by Matt Kaplan
Monster High Lisi Harrison	HP Should Have Died Mugglenet by Spartz
Necromancing the Stone Lisa McBride	Mythmaker: JK Rowling Amy Sickles
Valkyrie Rising Ingrid Paulson	Defiance CJ Redwine
The White Forest Adam McOmber	Part Wild Cerridwen Terrill
My Mother Was Nuts Penny Marshall	The Great Partnership Jonathan Sacks
Someone Like Adele Caroline Sanderson	Into the Fire Dakota Meyer

So Rich, So Poor
Peter Elderman

The Feminist and the Cowboy
Alisa Valdes

Weird Things Customers Say in
Bookstores by Jen Campbell

Adele
Sarah Louise James

Dead in Dallas
Charlene Harris

Dead Until Dark
Charlene Harris

Shit My Dad Says
Justin Halpren

High on Arrival
McKenzie Phillips

14 Steps to Awaken the
Sacred Feminine by Norton

In Praise of Messy Lives
Katie Rolphie

Etiquette and Espionage
Gail Carriger

The Dirty Girls Social Club
Alisa Valdes-Rodriguez

Playing with Boys
Alisa Valdes-Rodriguez

Make Him Look Good
Alisa Valdes-Rodriguez

Almost Moon
Alice Seabold

The House of Seven Gables
Nathaniel Hawthorne

American Isis: Sylvia Plath
Carl Rollyson

Lincoln: Vampire Hunter
Seth Graham-Smith

The King Maker's Daughters
Phillipa Gregory

Born Again: Journals
Susan Sontag

A Jury of Her Peers
Elaine Showalter

Here I Go Again
Jen Lancaster

The Spindlers
Lauren Oliver

Tales of Beedle the Bard
JK Rowling

Tough Shit: Life Advice
Kevin Smith

The Wizard's Daughter
Catherine Coulter

The Lord of Darkness
Elizabeth Hoyt

Birdwing
Rafe Martin

Anti-Fragile
Nassim Taleb

Vagina: A New Biography
Naomi Wolf

Perks of Being A Wallflower
Stephen Chobsky (Again)

Lucky Me: A Memoir
Sachi Parker

Blindspot
Banjaji and Greenwald

All Together Dead
Charlaine Harris (Again)

The Vampire and the Virgin
Kerrelynn Sparks (Again)

Bossypants
Tina Fey

The Lost History of the Little People
Susan B Martinez

The End of Childhood
Arthur C Clarke (Kindle)

Anais Nin: The Last Days
Barbara Kraft (Kindle)

Argo
Antonio Mendez

Pure
Juliana Baggott

Fuse
Juliana Baggott

Warm Bodies
Marion Isaac

World War Z
Max Brooks

Dead Ever After
Charlaine Harris

The Silver Linings Play Book
Mathew Quick

The Last Dragon
Silvana De Mari

Cloud Atlas
David Mitchell

The Story (Poetry)
Michael Ondaatje

The Collage of Dreams
Sharon Spencer (Again)

The Mirror and the Garden
Evelyn J Hintz (Again)

Alchemy and Kabbalah
Gershome Scholem

The Antidote
Oliver Burkeman

Unbearable Light: A Memoir
Portia de Rossi

Nowhere But Home
Liza Palmer

Storm of Swords (Again)
George R.R. Martin

Game of Thrones (Again)
George R.R. Martin

Dance of Dragons (Again)
George R.R. Martin

Drinking With Men
Rosie Schapp

Truth in Advertising
John Kennedy

Shitty Mom: Parenting Guide
Kilmartin, Moline, Ybarbo

Homesick: A Memoir
Sela Ward

Shambala Principle
Sakyong Mipham

How To Be an Adult In
Love by David Richo

The Life of Pi
Yann Martel

Into Darkness: Star Trek
Alan Dean Foster

A Million Suns
Beth Revis

Shades of Earth
Beth Revis

The Red Glass
Laura Rasu

Dragon Rider (To Ana)
Cornelia Funke

Ghost Written
David Mitchell

The Tragedy Paper
Elizabeth Leban

Kiss of a Vampire
Cynthia Garner

Code
Kathy Rieches

I Couldn't Love You More
Jillian Medoff

Huger Point
Jillian Medoff

Club Dead
Charlene Harris

The Vampires in the Lemon Grove
Karen Russell

Swampland!
Karen Russell

My Heart Lies South
Elizabeth Borton de Trevino

On The Map
Simon Garfield

A Shining Affliction
Annie G Rogers, PhD

My Horizontal Life
Chelsea Handler

The Impossible Cube
Steven Halperin

Beyond The Wall: Fire & Ice
Ed James Lowder

My Boyfriend Wrote A Book
About Me by Hilary Winston

Diary of a Submissive
Sophie Morgan

A Lamp in the Darkness
Jack Kornfield

Down the Up Escalator
Barbara Garson

Beyond Belief: Scientology
Jenna Miscavige Hill

Ethical Slut (Again)
Easton and Hardy

American Gun: A History
Chris Kyle

Past Lives For Beginners
Douglas De Long

12 Shades of Surrender
Harlequin Anthology

St Lucy's Home for Girls Raised by
Wolves by Karen Russell

The Heist by Janet Evanovich
And Lee Goldberg

Under The Light
Laura Whitcomb

Always Watching
Chevy Stevens

Four and Twenty Blackbirds
Cherie Priest (Again)

The Girl with the Iron Touch
Katy Cross

Towering
Alex Flinn

Bewitching
Alex Flinn

The Changeling
Phillipa Gregory

Stormbringers
Phillipa Gregory

The White Princess
Phillipa Gregory

Poison Princess
Kresley Cole

Storm Front
Richard Castle

I'm Not Gonna Lie To You
George Lopez

The Creation of Anne Boleyn
Susan Bordo

Anna Dressed in Blood
Kendare Black

Names for the Sea: Strangers
in Iceland by Sarah Moss

Chasing the Sun
Richard Cohen

Physics of the Impossible
Micko Kaku

Tesla: Inventor of the
Electrical Age by Carlson

Blood and Beauty: Borgias
Sarah Dunn

The Ice Princess (Swedish)
Camilla Lackberg

The Women of the Cousin's
War by Phillipa Gregory

The Tender Solider
Vanessa Gezari

Lost Bones
Kathy Rieches

I Wear the Black Hat
Chuck Klosterman

NOS4A2
Joe Hill

Everything Is Perfect When
You Are a Liar Kelly Oxford

The Inexplicables
Cherie Priest (Again)

Andalusian Friend
Alexander Soderberg

The Teleportation Accident
Ned Beauman

The Immortal Life of
Henrietta Lacks by Skloot

Empire Antarctica
Gavin Francis

Improbably Scholars
David L Kirp

Nine Years Under
Sheri Booker

Pieces of Light
Charles Fennyhough

Permanent Present Tense
Susan Corkin

The Bone Season
Samantha Shannon

The Ocean at the End of the Lane
Neil Gaiman

The Third Kingdom
Terry Goodkind

Kate: The Future Queen
Kate Nichol

The Wolves of Midwinter
Anne Rice

Wild
Cheryl Strayed

Dies the Fire
SM Sterling

Death of the Liberal Class
Chris Hedges

Vanished
Wil S Hylton

All I Want For Christmas Is
A Vampire by Kerrelynn Sparks
Spellbound
Sylvia Day

Mirages: 1939-1947
Anais Nin

Dirty Love
Andre Dubus III

The New And Poisonous Air
Adam McOmber

Fathom
Cherie Priest

Where Did You See Her
Last? Lemony Snicket

S. (The Ship Theseus)
JJ Abrams and Doug Dorst

For Darkness Shows The
Stars by Diane Peterfreund

Across A Star-Swept Sea
Diane Peterfreund

Courtesies and Conspiracies
Gail Carriger

Fiddlehead
Cherie Priest

The Werewolf's Guide To
Life by Ritch Duncan

The Surf Guru
Doug Dorst

Heat of the Night
Sylvia Day

Entwined in You
Sylvia Day

Reflected in You
Sylvia Day

The Queen is Dead
Kate Locke

Black and Blue
Gena Showalter

Emma
Jane Austen

Mansfield Park
Jane Austen

Northanger Abby
Jane Austen

Persuasion
Jane Austen

Pride and Prejudice
Jane Austen

Sense and Sensibility
Jane Austen

Elizabeth of York
Alison Weir

Simple Dreams (Memoir)
Linda Ronstadt

The Reason I Jump
Naoki Higashida

Thanks for Your Service
David Finkle

I Am Malala
Malala Yousafazai

Size Matters Not
Warwick Davis

Ordeal
Linda Lovelace

The Invention of Wings
Sue Monk Kidd

Anti-Fragile (Again)
Nassim Nicholas Taleb

Twilight Eyes
Dean Koontz

Long Live The Queen
Kate Locke

God Save The Queen
Kate Locke

Diary of a Submissive
Sophie Morgan (Again)

Zealot
Raza Aslan

The Shores of Knowledge
Joyce Applebee

Pirates of the Time Stream
Stephen White

What If
Shirley MacLaine

A Captain and a Corset
Mary Wine

Breath Iron
Kate Cross

Heart of Brass
Kate Cross

Touch of Steel
Kate Cross

A Lady Can Never Be Too Curious
Mary Wine

William Shakespeare's Star Wars
Ian Doescher

Brain on Fire
Susannah Cahalan (Again)

Notes from the Underbelly
Risa Greene (Again)

Tales from the Crib
Risa Greene (Again)

A Government of Wolves
John W Whitehead

My Stroke of Insight
Jill Bolte Taylor PhD.

The Richest Man in Babylon
George S Clason

The Golden Compass and Philosophy
Ed by Greene and Robinson

24 and Philosophy
Ed by Reed

Trueblood and Philosophy
Ed by Dunn and Housel

Watchmen and Philosophy
Ed Mark D White

Superman and Philosophy
Ed Mark D White

Led Zeppelin and Philosophy
Ed by Scott Calef

Superman and Philosophy
Ed by Mark D White

Emily Dickinson and Philosophy
Ed by Deppman, Noble and Stonum

Sons of Anarchy and Philosophy
Ed by George A Dunn

The Walking Dead and Philosophy
Ed Mark D White

Sharp Objects
Gillian Flynn

Striking Distance
Pamela Clare

Breaking Point
Pamela Clare

Extreme Exposure
Pamela Clare

Hard Evidence
Pamela Clare

As Cool As I Am
Peter Fromm

Fury
Koren Zailckas

Artist, Philosopher, Warrior
Paul Strathern

Secrets of Mary Magdalene
Ed Burstein and Keijzer

Ashes, Ashes
Rene Barhavel

Angel, Angel
April Stevens

The Truth Is
Melissa Etheridge

Gone Girl
Gillian Flynn

Gone Baby Gone
Dennis Lehane

Labor Day
Joyce Maynard

Encounters with Flying
Humanoids by Gerhard

The Road
Cormac McCarthy

Midnight Crossroads
Charlaine Harris

Loneliness
Cacioppo & Patrick

The Fault in Our Stars
John Green

How To Seduce A Vampire
Kerrelynn Sparks

This Land is Their Land
Barbara Ehrenreich

Actor's Anonymous
James Franco

Palo Alto
James Franco

China Dolls
Lisa See

A Shiver of Light
Laurel K Hamilton

The English Major
Jim Harrison

Top Secret 21
Janet Evanovich

Linger
Viggo Mortensen

Coincidence of Memory
Viggo Mortensen

Miyelo
Viggo Mortensen

Severed Souls
Terry Goodkind

Ten Big Ones (Again)
Janet Evanovich

Deadlocked
Charlaine Harris (Again)

Collages
Anais Nin (Again)

City of Heavenly Fire
Cassandra Clare

Red Winter
Clark Hayes

I Explain A Few Things
Pablo Neruda

The Fall of the Governor P1
Kirkman and Bonansinga

The Battle For Wonderla
Toni Diterlizzi

The Vampire With The Dragon
Tattoo by Kerrilynn Sparks

The Fall of the Governor P2
Kirkman and Bonansinga

The Good Luck of Right Now
Mathew Quick

Living With A Wild God
Barbara Ehenreich

Gobekli Tepe
Andrew Collins

Odysseus in America
Jonathan Shay, MD PHD

Wave
Sondali Deraniyagala

Visions in Death
J.D. Robb

Redemption Unmasked
LJ Smith (Vampire Diaries)

Plum Lucky (Again)
Janet Evanovich

Elven on Top (Again)
Janet Evanovich

Bloodshot (Again)
Cherie Priest

The People's History
Howard Zinn

Jungleland
Christopher S Steward

Spiderbones (Again)
Kathy Reiches

Orange Is The New Black
Piper Kerman

A Certain Slant of Light
Laura Whitcomb (Again)

Eat, Pray, Love (Again)
Elizabeth Gilbert

Fair Game (Again)
Valerie Plame Wilson

Dark Forces
Kenneth R Timmerman

Mom's Night Out
Tricia Goyer

Another Day On the Frontal Lobe
Katrina Firlik (Again)

That Night
Chevy Steven

The Claiming of Sleeping Beauty
Anne Rice (Again)

Beauty's Punishment
Anne Rice (Again)

Dark Lycan
Christine Feehan

Dark Wolves
Christine Feehan

The Book Thief
Markus Zusak

Boneshaker (Again)
Cherie Priest

Dreadnought (Again)
Cherie Priest

The Inexplicables(Again)
Cherie Priest

Dark Blood
Christine Feehan

If I Stay
Gayle Forman

Where She Went
Gayle Forman

The Awakening
LJ Smith (Again)

The Struggle
LJ Smith (Again)

The Fury
LJ Smith (Again)

Dark Reunion
LJ Smith (Again)

Beauty's Release
Anne Rice (Again)

The Wolf Gift
Anne Rice (Again)

The Wolves of Midwinter
Anne Rice (Again)

The King's Curse
Phillipa Gregory

The 100
Kass Morgan

A Wrinkle in Time
Madeline L'Engle (Again)

A Wind In The Door
Madeline L'Engle (Again)

A Swiftly Tilting Planet
Madeline L'Engle (Again)

An Acceptable Time
Madeline L'Engle (Again)

Reading List 2015

Sarah Cannery
Karen Joy Fowler

All The Light We Cannot See
Anthony Doerr

Waistcoats and Weaponry
Gail Carriger

Deadly Heat
Richard Castle

The Drop
Dennis Lehane

Necessary Lie
Diane Chamberlain

A Cold Lonely Place
Sara J Henry

Learning to Swim
Sara J Henry

A Discovery of Witches
Deborah Harkness

The Kill Order
James Dashner

The Scorch Trials
James Dashner

The Death Cure
James Dashner

The End of Absence
Michael Harris

A Cup of Water Under My Bed
Daisy Hernandez

A Spool of Blue Thread
Anne Tyler

The Angel Experiment
James Patterson (Max Ride)

School's Out Forever
James Patterson (Max Ride)

Saving The World
James Patterson (Max Ride)

Outlander
Diane Gabledon

Drums in Autumn
Diane Gabledon

Voyager
Diane Gabledon

Gambles Mill: Proof
Cari Lynn Vaughn

The Epic of Xanthy: Proof
Cari Lynn Vaughn

Freedom For Celestria: Proof
Cari Lynn Vaughn

The Kaleen: Proof
Cari Lynn Vaughn

Emotions: Proof
Cari Lynn Vaughn

Heaven's Home: Proof
Cari Lynn Vaughn

Unzipped and Undone: Proof
Cari Lynn Vaughn

Flying Free: Proof
Cari Lynn Vaughn

A Fortunate Curse: Proof
Cari Lynn Vaughn

There Was A Little Girl
Brooke Shields (Bio)

True Love (Bio)
Jennifer Lopez

A Religion of One's Own
Thomas Moore

Belle
Paula Byrne

Elegies For The Brokenhearted
Christie Hodgen

Resilience
Jessie Close and Pete Early

Girl of Nightmares
Kendare Blake

Anti-goddess
Kendare Blake

Still Alice
Lisa Genova

Left Neglected
Lisa Genova

Love Anthony
Lisa Genova

Flashforward (Again)
Robert J Sawyer

The Ghost Line
Elementary Tie-In

Mother Tongue (Again)
Bill Bryson

Beauty's Kingdom
Anne Rice

The Girl On The Train
Paula Hawks

Homecoming: The 100
Kass Morgan

Legal Research and Writing
Textbook by Bast and Hawkings

The World Is A Stage
Cari Lynn Vaughn (Proof)

The Long Hot Summer
Cari Lynn Vaughn (Proof)

The Long Road
Cari Lynn Vaughn (Proof)

Monc No Aware
Cari Lynn Vaughn (Proof)

Wings of Desire
Cari Lynn Vaughn (Proof)

Sous Rature
Cari Lynn Vaughn (Proof)

Such A Pretty Fat
Jen Lancaster (Again)

Day Shift
Charlene Harris

Sappho's Leap
Erica Jong (Again)

The Giver
Louis Lowry

Not That Kind of Girl
Lena Dunham

The Explosive Child
Ross Greene

Serena
Ron Rash

Healthy Brain, Happy Brain
Wendy Suzuki

Indiana Jones and Army of the Dead
Steve Perry

The Scam
Janet Evanovich

These Girls
Chevy Stevens

Library of Souls
Ransom Riggs

Moyers on America
Bill Moyers

Dark Ghost
Christine Feehan

Speaking in Bones
Kathy Reiches

Jack of Spades
Joyce Carol Oates

The Dark Half
Stephen King

Forever
Pete Hamill

Prudence
Gail Carriger

Sidewalk Oracles
Robert Moss

The Martian
Andy Weir

Fear of Dying
Erica Jong

Love Never Fails
Mathew Quick

Decentered Proof
Cari Lynn Vaughn

Desideratum Proof
Cari Lynn Vaughn

Grok Proof
Cari Lynn Vaughn

The Couch Critic
Cari Lynn Vaughn

Sehnsucht Proof
Cari Lynn Vaughn

Forza Del Destino Proof
Cari Lynn Vaughn

Gnosis Proof
Cari Lynn Vaughn

I Regret Nothing
Jen Lancaster

From this Moment On
Shania Twain

A Fine Romance
Candace Bergan

Masters of Sex
Thomas Maier

The Science Happily Ever After
Ty Tashiro

Literary Lost (Again)
Sarah Stuart Clarke

Living Lost
J Wood (Again)

The Omnivore's Dilemma
Michael Pollen (Again)

The Art of War
Sun Tzu

Government Zero
Michael Savage

Troublemaker
Leah Remini

Wildflower
Drew Barrymore

The Knight of the Seven Kingdoms
GRR Martin

Seven Years To Sin
Sylvia Day

Fates and Furies
Lauren Groff

The Sorcerer's Stone
JK Rowling (Again)

Heir to the Empire
Timothy Zahn (Again)

Lost in Hypertext Proof
Cari Lynn Vaughn

Legal Writing
Textbook

Fire In the Mind (Again)
George Johnson

Field Methods in Archeology
Hester, Shafter, Feder

Why Not Me?
Mindy Kaling

Of Monsters and Madness
Jessica Verday

Warheart
Terry Goodkind

Lights Out
Ted Koppel

The Mystery of the Crystal Skulls
Morton and Thomas

The Quantum Thief
Hannu Rajaniemi

The Fractal Prince
Hannu Rajaniemi

The Causal Angel
Hannu Rajaniemi

The Bustline Special
Mike Reznik

The Man without a Shadow
Joyce Carol Oats

The Force Awakens
Alan Dean Foster

Marriage Confidential
Pamela Haag

Why Is This Night Different From All
Other Nights? By Lemony Snicket

Nostromo
Joseph Conrad

Lost in Hypertext Proof
Cari Lynn Vaughn

Purple Rose of Zurzu Proof
Cari Lynn Vaughn

To Remember Proof
Cari Lynn Vaughn

Beyond In Too Deep Proof
Cari Lynn Vaughn

Tuykame Proof
Cari Lynn Vaughn

From Acheron Proof
Cari Lynn Vaughn

A Brief History of Time
Stephen Hawking (Again)

Living In the Light
Shakti Gawain (Again)

Bird by Bird
Anne Lamott (Again)

Origins
Neil deGrasse Tyson

The Big Questions: Faith & Science
Alistair McGrath

Torts Personal Injury Law Textbook
Statsky

Academic Writing (Instructor)
Behrens and Rosen

Longman Writer (Instructor)
Nadell and Langan

Cari's Books
As of October 2002

The Goblin Market and Other Poems by Christina Rossetti
A Night without Armor by Jewel
The American Night by Jim Morrison
Handwriting by Michael Ondaatje
German Romantic Poetry
The Vagina Monologues by Eve Ensler
Iona Moon by Melanie Rae Thon
Exposure by Katherine Harris
Walking to Mercury by Starhawk
Acts of Love by Maureen Daly
A Time to Choose by Janine Boissard
A Matter of Feeling by Janine Boissard
Local Girls by Alice Hoffman
White Oleander by Janet Fitch
Virgin Suicides by Jeffery Eugenides
Snow Falling on Cedars by David Gutterson
Where the Heart Is by Billie Letts
Heat and Dust by Ruth Prowler Jhabvala
Shipping News E. Annie Proloux
Solo Variations by Cassandra Garbus
The Genius of Affection by Marilyn Sides
Shanghai Baby by Wei Hui
The Secret Life of Bees by Sue Monk Kidd
Girl Interrupted by Susanna Kaysen
Prozac Nation by Elizabeth Wurtzel
Mothman Prophesies by John A. Keel
The Unbearable Lightness of Being by Milan Kundra
Holder of the World by Bharati Mukherjee
Legends of the Fall by Jim Harrison
Fall of the Sparrow by Robert Hellenga
Amy and Isabelle by Elizabeth Stout
The Hottest State by Ethan Hawk
Foxfire by Joyce Carol Oates
Will You Always Love Me? Joyce Carol Oates
In the Skin of the Lion by Ondaatje
The English Patient by Ondaatje
Running in The Family by Ondaatje
Anil's Ghost by Ondaatje
Tropic of Orange by Karen Tei Yamashiti
The Stranger by Albert Camus
No Exit and Other Plays by Sartre

Nausea and The Wall by Sartre
Gargoyles by Thomas Bernhard
Cassandra by Christa Wolf
Quest for Christa T. by Christa Wolf
Damage by Josephine Hart
Ariel by Sylvia Plath
The Bell Jar by Sylvia Plath
Dorothy Parker's Short Stories and Poetry
Liars Club by Mary Karr
The Kiss by Katherine Harris
Lizard by Banana Yoshimoto
Kitchen by Banana Yoshimoto
The Bridges of Madison County by James Waller
Herland and Selected Stories by Charlotte Perkins Gilman
House of the Spirits by Isabelle Allende
A Portrait of the Artist by James Joyce
Sylvia Beach and the Lost Generation by Noel Riley Fitch
Ordinary Miracles Poems by Erica Jong
What Women Want by Erica Jong
Fear of Flying by Erica Jong
Devil At Large by Erica Jong
Tropic Of Cancer by Henry Miller
Henry and June by Anais Nin
Journal of Incest by Anais Nin
Journal of Fire by Anais Nin
Delta of Venus by Anais Nin
A Spy in the House of Love Anais Nin
House of Incest by Anais Nin
Under A Glass Bell by Anais Nin
Cities of the Interior by Anais Nin
Anais Nin and the Remaking of Self by Richard-Allerdyce
Diary Volume 1 by Anais Nin
Diary Volume 2 by Anais Nin
Diary Volume 3 by Anais Nin
Diary Volume 4 by Anais Nin
Diary Volume 5 by Anais Nin
Diary Volume 6 by Anais Nin
Diary Volume 7 by Anais Nin
In Favor of the Sensitive Man and other essays by Anais Nin
D.H. Lawrence, An Unprofessional Study by Anais
Anais Nin: An Introduction by Franklin and Schneider
Anais: An Erotic Life by Sylvia Beach
Anais Nin: Deidre Bair
Anais Nin Reader edited by Philip K. Jason

A Literate Passion: Letters from Nin and Miller
Anais Nin Narratives Edited by Salvatore
Nightwood: Dejuna Barnes
Rimbaud: Poems
In the Time of the Assassins by Henry Miller
Sexus by Henry Miller
Plexus by Henry Miller
Nexus by Henry Miller
The Romance of Tristan and Iseult
Wuthering Heights by Emily Bronte
The Wuthering Heights Handbook
Jane Eyre by Charlotte Bronte
Tenant of Wildfell Hall by Anne Bronte
Shirley by Charlotte Bronte
Eugene Grant by Balzac
The Metamorphosis by Kafka
Dracula by Bram Stoker
Reflections on Dracula by Elizabeth Miller
Anna Karenina by Tolstoy
The Goddess and Other Women by Joyce Carol Oates
A World Of Pies by Karen Stolz
Hot Six Janet Evanonvich
Zoya by Danielle Steele
Dwelling in the Gray by Clay Harvey
White Lies by Anna Salter (Strip)
Everybody Dies by Lawrence Block (Strip)
Gravity by Tess Gerritson (Strip)
The Rising Sun by Michael Crichton
The Firm by John Grisham
The Pelican Brief by John Grisham
Sphinx by Robin Cook
Bless the Child by Catherine Cash Spellman (Strip)
The Mammoth Hunters
Fin McCool by Morgan Llywelyn
Grania by Morgan Llywelyn
Druids by Morgan Llywelyn
Bard by Morgan Llywelyn
Horse Goddess by Morgan Llywelyn
Silverland by Nancy Harding
She Who Remembers by Linda Laye Shuler
Voice of the Eagle by Linda Laye Shuler
Women of the Mists Lynn Armistead McKee
Touches the Stars by Lynn Armistead McKee
Keeper of Dreams by Lynn Armistead McKee

Walks in Stardust by Lynn Armistead McKee
Prince of Tides by Par Conroy
Beaches by Iris Rainer Dart
Joy Luck Club by Amy Tan
Katherine by Achee Min
Necessary Parties by Barbara Dana
The Power of One by Bruce Courtney
The Lias Marie of France
Age of Innocence by Edith Wharton
Ethan Fromm by Edith Wharton
A Farewell to Arms by Hemmingway
The Old Man and the Sea by Hemmingway
A Moveable Feast by Hemmingway
Phantom of the Opera by Gaston Leroux
Hunchback of Nortre Dame by Victor Hugo
A Time in Between by Shirley Streshinsky
Dances with Wolves William Blake
Goonies by James Kahn
ET by William Kotzwinkle
Dune by Frank Hubert
Star Wars by George Lucas
Empire Strikes Back by Donald F. Glut
Return of the Jedi by James Kahn
Splinter of the Minds Eye by Alan Dean Foster
Far and Away by Sonja Massie
Fatal Attraction by H.B. Gilmour
Sliver by Ira Levin
Wish you a Merry Murder by Valerie Wolzien
Shoeless Joe Jackson WP Kinsella
Home for the Holidays by Chris Radiant
Robin Hood: Prince of Thieves by Simon Green
Thunderheart by Lowell Charters
Postcards from the Edge by Carrie Fisher
Heartbeat by Norma Fox Mazer and Harry Mazer
Dune by Frank Herbert
The Mists of Avalon by Marion Zimmer Bradley
Encounters at Farpoint by David Gerrold
Imzadi by Peter David
Q-in-law by Peter David
Princess Bride by William Goldman
Beyond Another Door by Sonia Levin
Dharma Bums by Jack Keroac
An Acceptable Time by Madeleine L'Engle
Quantum Leap: Too Close For Comfort by Ashley McConnell

Ground Zero by Kevin J. Anderson
Fight the Future by Elizabeth Hand
Braveheart by Randal Wallace
Raiders of the Lost Ark by Campbell Black
Temple of Doom by James Kahn
Last Crusade by Rob MacGregor
Peril at Delphi by Rob MacGregor
Seven Veils by Rob MacGregor
Dance of the Giants by Rob MacGregor
Unicorn's Legacy by Rob MacGregor
Interior World by Rob MacGregor
The Fury by L.J. Smith
The Struggle by L.J. Smith
Dracula by Fred Saberhagen and James V. Hart
Lord of the Vampires by Jean Kalogridis
Interview with A Vampire by Anne Rice
Lestat the Vampire by Anne Rice
Tale of the Body Thief by Anne Rice
Memenoch the Devil by Anne Rice
Violin by Anne Rice
Belinda by Anne Rice
The Mummy by Anne Rice
Merrick by Anne Rice (Strip)
Prism: Bio of Anne Rice by Kathryn Ramsland
Who Walks by Moonlight by Marjorie McEvoy
Odyssey by Homer
Iliad by Homer
Metamorphose by Ovid
The Art of Love by Ovid
The Neverending Story by Michael Ende
Light a Single Candle Beverly Butler
Wait for what will come by Barbara Michaels
Search the Shadows by Barbara Michaels
Gentle Rouge by Johanna Lindsey
Ice and Fire by Connie Mason
Brave New Land by Connie Mason
Wild Promise, Sweet Promise by Janelle Taylor
Last Viking Queen by Janelle Taylor
Surrender my Love by Johanna Lindsey
Surrender by Emily Carmichael
Eyes of The Night by Diane Bane
Just Friends by Norma Klein
Fools by Pat Cadigan
Magic Kingdom For Sale by Terry Brooks

The Black Unicorn by Terry Brooks
Willow by Wayland Drew
Virtual Mode by Anthony Pierce
Conspiracy Theory by J.H. Marks
The Hobbit by J.R.R. Tolkin
Lord of The Rings by J.R.R,. Tolkin
The Towers by J.R.R. Tolkin
The Return of The King by J.R.R. Tolkin
Red Bird of Ireland by Sondra Gorden Langford
Circle in the Sea by Steve Senn (Out of Print)
Circle of Time by Margaret J. Anderson
The Kings Fifth by Scott O'Dell
The Captive by Scott O'Dell (Out of Print)
The Feathered Serpent by Scott O'Dell (Out of Print)
The Amethyst Ring by Scott O'Dell (Out of Print)
Casilda of the Rising Moon by Elizabeth Borton de Trevino (Out of Print)
Cat's Magic by Margaret Greaves (Out of Print)
A Room of Ones Own by Virginia Woolf
Long Day's Journey into Night by Eugene O'Neill
Buoyant Billions by George Bernard Shaw (Out of Print)
George Bernard Shaw's Plays
Caesar and Cleopatra by Shaw
Arms and The Man by G.B. Shaw
Pygmalion by G.B. Shaw
Hedda Gabber by Ibsen
Doll's House by Ibsen
Julie by August Strindberg
Hands Around by Arthur Schnitzler
Important of Being Ernest by Oscar Wilde
The Playboy of The Western World
Cherry Orchard by Chekov
Three Sisters by Chekov
The Birth of Tragedy by Nietzsche
Plato's Dialogues
Plato's Cratylus
Sherlock Holmes by Doyle
The Haunting by Shirley Jackson
Death in Venice by Thomas Mann
Frankenstein by Mary Shelly
Leaves of Grass by Walt Whitman
The Scarlet Letter by Hawthorne
A Connecticut Yankee in King Arthur's Court by Mark Twain
Great Expectations by Charles Dickens
The Tell-Tale Heart and Other Stories by Poe

Complete Tales of Edgar Alan Poe
Candide by Voltaire
Madam Bovary by Flaubert
As You Like It by Shakespeare
The Late Romances by Shakespeare
Antony and Cleopatra by Shakespeare
Macbeth by Shakespeare
Much Ado About Nothing by Shakespeare
King Lear by Shakespeare
Henry IV part 1 and 2 by Shakespeare
Henry V by Shakespeare
Hamlet by Shakespeare
The Taming of the Shrew by Shakespeare
The Tempest by Shakespeare
Midsummer Night's Dream by Shakespeare
Othello by Shakespeare
Measure for Measure by Shakespeare
Bedford Companion to Shakespeare
Canterbury Tales by Chaucer
Niblungenlied Penguin Classics
Beowulf and other old English Poems
Prince of Annwn by Evangeline Walton
Lady of the Lake by Tennyson
Oedipus the King by Sophocles
All Quiet on The Western Front by Erich Maria Remarque
Gulliver's Travels by Jonathan Swift
Idles of The King by Sir Walter Scott
To Kill A Mocking Bird by Harper Lee
Sons and Lovers by D.H. Lawrence
Women in Love by D.H.L
The Rainbow by D.H.L
Lady Chatterley's Lover by D.H.L
Three Guineas by Virginia Woolf
Orlando by Virginia Woolf
To The Lighthouse by Virginia Woolf
The Haunted House and Other Short Stories by Virginia Woolf
Mrs. Dalloway by Virginia Woolf
Like Water for Chocolate by Laura Esquirel
Love Story by Erik Segal
Peel My Love Like an Onion by Ana Castilo
Juneteenth by Ralph Waldo Ellison
Herzog by Saul Bellow
Feminine Mystic Betty Friedan
Honest Courtesan by Margaret Rosetheau

Selected Poems and Letters by Veronica Franco
Currency of Eros by Ann Rosalind Jones
The Hero with a Thousand Faces by Joseph Campbell
The Art of the Novel by Milan Kundra
A Course in Linguistics Saussure
Prisonhouse Language James
Of Grammatology by Derrida
On the Kabbalah and Criticism by Scholem
Poetry, Language and Thought by Heidegger
Ficcones by Jorge Luis Borges
After Babel by George Steiner
Inwardness and Theater in the English Renaissance by Maus
Know it All Literature by Sean Francis
Literature and its Writers
Fiction Workshop Companion by Jon Volkmer
Novels into Film by George Bluestone
Well-Stocked Book Case
Model Student Essays
How to Read and Write Fiction
French Textbooks (3)
Philosophy Text Book
History of African Archaeology and Art
Critical Issues in Contemporary Culture by Christopher Gould
The 29 Most Common Writing Mistakes
The Literature Teacher's Book of Lists
Literature as Exploration by Louise M. Rosenblatt
Writer's Inc.
MLA Guide to Writing Research Papers
Models for Clear Writing by Donald
Communication Works by Gamble
Do the Write Thing
How to Get Happily Published
Writer's Market 1999
Transformation and Text by Steven Joyce
Elements of Style
A Short Introduction to Literary Theory by Jonathan Cullers
Rewriting by Christian Moraru
Anatomy of Criticism by Northrop Frye
Two or Three Things I Know For Sure by Dorothy Allison
Helen Cixous
Born for Liberty
Written by Herself
A Book of Women Poets from Antiquity to Now edited by Barnstone
Feminisms edited by Warhol

Writing on the Body edited by Convoy, Medina and Standby
How to Suppress Women's Writing by Joanna Russ
Women in the 19th Century by Margaret Fuller (Dover Edition)
Soft Canons by Karen Kilcup
19th Century American Women Writers edited by Karen Kilcup
19th Century American Women Writers, A Critical Reader edited by Kilcup
Literary Research Guide 3ed Edition
Norton Anthology of Literature Written by Women
Norton Introduction to Poetry
Bedford Reader
Initiation
St. Martin's Handbook
Anguished English
War and Peace in the Global Village
Common Culture
Aspects of Western Civilization
Hitler and Nazi Germany
Before the Deluge
Reunification
The Hiding Place by Corrie Ten Boom
Celtic Wisdom
The Age of Manipulation
Wisdom of the Ancients
Anthropology
Modern Drama in Theory and Practice part 2
Environmental Movement in Germany by Dominic
20,000 Baby Names
Distant Mirror
Lost Realms
Mythology
The Maya
Ancient Engineers
Silent Spring by Rachel Carson
The History of Western Philosophy by Bertrand Russell
The Mind of India
The Book of Questions
Portable Life 101
The Wounded Woman by Linda Schierse Leonard
Spiral Dance by Starhawk
A Path with Heart by Jack Kornfield
Path of Love by Deepak Chopra
The Art of Loving by Eric Fromm
Loving Each Other by Leo Buscaglia
Love by Leo Buscaglia

You Can Heal Your Life by Louise L. Hay
Living in the Light by Shakti Gawain
The Path of Transformation by Shakti Gawain
Ecstasy in an New Frequency by Chris Griscom
Don't Fall of the Mountain by Shirley MacLaine
Out On A Limb by Shirley MacLaine
Dancing in the Light by Shirley MacLaine
It's All in The Playing by Shirley MacLaine
Going Within by Shirley MacLaine
Dance While You Can by Shirley MacLaine
The Camino: A Journey of the Spirit by MacLaine
The Destiny of Man by Edgar Cayce
Encore Province by Peter Mayle
Couplehood by Paul Riser
Uh-Oh by Robert Fulgulm
All I Need to Know I Learned in Kindergarten by Fulgulm
The Dancing Wu-Li Masters by Gary Zukav
The User Illusion by Tor Norretranders
The Physics of Consciousness by Evan Harris Walker
The Simpson's and Philosophy edited Edwin
Adventures of Luke Skywalker by Galipeau
The Song of God
Siddhartha by Herman Hesse
The Lost Teachings of Jesus Christ
Uncover Your Past Lives
Coming Back by Dick Sutphan
Life After Life by Raymond Moody
Finding Your Answers Within by Dick Sutphan
How to Stay Alive In The Woods
Backpacking
The Kama Sutra
The Doors of Perception by Aldous Huxley
Introduction to Psychoanalysis by Freud
The Interpretation of Dreams by Freud
Modern Man in Search of A Soul by Jung
Psychoanalysis in Literature by Ruitenbeck
Gabriel Marcel's Perspectives on The Broken World by Hanley
The Existential Imagination by Carl/Hamalin
Myth of Sisyphus by Camus
Brilliant Madness by Patty Duke
Necessary Losses by Judith Vorist
Generation Sex by Dr. Judy
The Idiots Guide to A Healthy Relationship by Dr. Judy
Beyond Freedom and Dignity by B.F. Skinner

Future Shock by Alvin Toffer
Yoga
Edible Wild Plants
Gospel of The Red Man
Wild Trail Food
English Lit of The 17th and 18th Centuries
How To Clean Practically Anything
Oxford Desk Dictionary and Thesaurus
Synonym Finder
Spanish/English Dictionary
French/ English Dictionary
German/English Dictionary
Office 97 Handbooks
Insight Guide To Peru
Along the Inca Road by Karen Muller
Jung's Dreams
Dictionary of Clichés
Women's Bodies, Women's Wisdom
Made from this Earth Celia Norwood
Synchronicity by Deike Begg
Alias: Declassified by Mark Cotta Vaz
A Separate Peace by John Knowles
House Made of Dawn by N. Scott Momaday
The Thorn Birds by McCullough

Stripped Books

Cybil Disobedience
The Phoenix
When Darkness Falls
Dying to Have Her
Star Wars: Episode 1
My So Called Life Goes On
In The Forest of The Night
Leonard Martin's Film Guide
1984 by Orwell
American Tragedy by Hardy
Crow's Lazarus Heart
Dialogues of Plato
Iliad by Homer
Odyssey by Homer
In The Shadow of the Gargoyle Edited by Kirpatrick
Tarot Cards
How to play Chess

Healing Herbal Remedies
Bantam Medical Dictionary
PDR Family Guide to Symptoms
Sister Carrie by Dreiser
Face to Face with the Unknown by Hansen Steiger
Midnight in the Ruby Bayou by Elizabeth Lowell
Year's Best Fantasy by David Hartman
Hugger Mugger by Robert B. Parker
Lost Soul's by Poppy Z. Brite
Eagle's Daughter by Judith Tarr
Out of Avalon by Jennifer Roberson
Samurai's Wife by Laura Rowland
Glimpses of the Moon by Edith Wharton
Philip Marlowe by Raymond Chandler
The Truth is Out There: The Official Guide to the X-Files
Arabian Nights adapted by Jack Zipes
Two Years Before The Mast by Richard Henry Dana Junior
How to Father A Successful Daughter by Nicky Marone
Parisian Frolics (erotica translated from French)
Eveline II (erotica)
The Compete Guide To Middle Earth edited by Robert Foster
Dogrun
Leonard Martin's 2003 Movie and Video Guide
Pan by Knut Hamsun
The Matrix and Philosophy Edited by William Irwin

Free Box at GTCC

Connections, Contexts and Possibilities by Stephen Murabito
Critical Thinking, Reading and Writing by Sylvan Barnet and Hugo Bedau
Explorations in Basic Writing by Audrey L. Reynolds
Paragraph Practice—The 7th edition—by Kathleen E. Sullivan
New Beginnings: Writing with Fluency by Diane Fitton and Barbara Warner
Introduction to Writing by Jean Reynolds

Free Books

A Treasury of American Literature Before 1800 edited by Davis Frederick Mott
A Treasury of American Literature After 1800 edited by Davis Frederick Mott
A Treasury of the World's Greatest Speeches edited by Houston Peterson
A Treasury of the Familiar edited by Ralph L. Woods
A Treasury of Philosophy edited by Dagobert D. Runes
A Treasury of Philosophy after 1600 edited by Dagobert D. Runes
A Treasury of the Essay edited by Homer C. Combs

Sister's of the Earth
Claiming the Highlander by Kinley MacGregor
The Twentieth Wife by Indu Sundaresan
Women who Run With Wolves by Clarissa Pinkola Estes, Ph.D.
Speed of Light by Elizabeth Rosner
The Snow Garden by Christopher Rice
Brother Wind by Sue Harrison
My Sister the Mood by Sue Harrison
Children of the Ice by Charlotte Prentiss
Grass Crown by Colleen McCullough
The Adventures of Tom Sawyer
Caribee by Thomas Hoover
Educational Psychology by Paula R. Rothsten
Educational Psychology Annual
Principles of Science (For Elementary School)
Uses of the University
Content and Reading (For Elementary School Teachers)
Official AOL Guide to the Internet
Doctor's Book of Home Remedies by Prevention
French Grammar Book 1929
Proceedings of the First International UFO Congress edited by Curtis G Fuller
We are not the First by Andrew Tomas
Not of this World edited by Peter Kolosimo
The Outer Space Connections by Alan Sally Landsburg
Atlantis Rising Brad Steiger
The Gold of the Gods by Erich Von Daniken
Inside the Flying Saucers by George Adamski
UFO's Exist by Paris Flammonde
The UFO Experience by James Allen Hynek
National Enquirer UFO Report
Close Encounters of the 3rd Kind a novel by Steven Speilberg
Return of the Native by Thomas Hardy
Understanding Media: The Extensions of Man by Marshal McLuhan
Prize Stories 1962 The O Henry Awards
La Condition Humaine by Malraux 1946 French Edition
Le Reine Morte by Montherlant 1947 French Edition

New Books 9/2/02

Lively Art of Writing
365 Love Poems
Claiming of Sleeping Beauty
Notes from the Underground by Dostoyevsky
Beyond Psychology by Otto Rank

American Literature by Surkey, Milton, Stern
Body Language by Fast
Academic Job Search Handbook
100 Great Opera's and their Stories

Other Voices, Other Vistas by Barbara A Solomon
Big Trouble by Dave Berry

Kids Books

The Dark Angel by Meredith Pierce
A Gathering of Gargoyles by Meredith Pierce

The Lion, the Witch and the Wardrobe by C.S. Lewis
Prince Caspian by C.S. Lewis
The Voyage of the Dawn Treader by C.S. Lewis
The Silver Chair by C.S. Lewis
The Horse and His Boy by C.S. Lewis
The Magician's Nephew by C.S. Lewis
The Last Battle by C.S. Lewis

The Wizard of Oz by L. Frank Baum
The Land of OZ by L. Frank Baum
Ozma of Oz by L. Frank Baum
Dorothy and the Wizard in Oz by L. Frank Baum
The Road to Oz by L. Frank Baum
The Emerald City of Oz by L. Frank Baum
The Patchwork Girl of Oz by L. Frank Baum
The Scarecrow of Oz by L. Frank Baum
Rinkitink in Oz by L. Frank Baum
The Lost Princess of Oz by L. Frank Baum
The Magic of Oz by L. Frank Baum
Glinda of Oz by L. Frank Baum
The Life of Santa Claus by L. Frank Baum

Anne of Green Gables by L.M. Montgomery
Anne of Avonlea by L.M. Montgomery
Anne of the Island by L.M. Montgomery
Anne of Windy Poplars by LM Montgomery
Anne of Ingleside by L.M. Montgomery
Rilla of Ingleside L.M. Montgomery

Emily of The New Moon by L.M. Montgomery
Kilmey of the Orchard by L.M. Montgomery

Zia by Scott O'Dell
Island of the Blue Dolphins by Scott O'Dell
Hatchet by Gary Paulson
The Witching of Ben Wagner
Children of the Dragon by Rose Estes
Shadow Castle
A Darker Magic
Dragons by Shirley Rousseau Murphy
Ivory Lyre by Shirley Rousseau Murphy
A Hidden Magic by Vivian Vande Velde
The Witch Herself Phyllis Reynolds Naylor
Witch Water by Phyllis Reynolds Naylor
Witch Sister by Phyllis Reynolds Naylor

Sweet Valley Double Jeopardy
Sweet Valley Deadly Summer
Sweet Valley Kidnapped #13
Sweet Valley On The Edge #40
Sweet Valley Deceptions #14
Caitlin True Love
Caitlin Loving
Caitlin Love Lost
Caitlin Together Forever
Caitlin Forever and Always

In the Forest of the Night by Amelia Atwater-Rhodes (Strip 1999)

Old Books That Might Be Worth Something
(Mom, Grandma and Great Grandma's)

Room For One More
By Anna Perrott Rose 1954

Tender is the Night by F Scott Fitzgerald
Charles Scribner and Sons 1962
This Side of Paradise by F Scott Fitzgerald
Charles Scribner and Sons
Great Gatsby by F Scott Fitzgerald
Charles Scribner and Sons
The Last Tycoon by F Scott Fitzgerald
Charles Scribner and Sons

Little Women by Louisa May Alcott
Nelson Doubleday 1950
Jo's Boy's by Louisa May Alcott
Nelson Doubleday
Under the Lilacs by Louisa May Alcott
Nelson Doubleday
Eight Cousins by Louisa May Alcott
Nelson Doubleday
Jack and Jill by Louisa May Alcott
Nelson Doubleday

American Wit and Humor by One Hundred of America's Leading Humorists
Joe Chandler was the author of the introduction, 1907 1st edition from New York
$52 if in great shape, $45 for decent condition

Cordelia: A Novel by Winston Graham. Doubleday 1949

East of Eden and The Wayward Bus
Stienbeck — Viking Press, 1952.
Only worth $5.95 as far as I can tell

Favorite Poems and Ballads of Rudyard Kipling
Pemberville Public Library copy from 1940
Worth $3-$15

Rebecca of Sunnybrook Farm
Kate Douglas Wiggin
Grosset and Dunlap, 1903 1st edition (not first?)
$450 if in excellent shape

Kings Cavalier $4-$6
Little Brown and Company, 1950?

Bold Robin Hood and His Outlaw Band
Louis Rhead Books, Incorporated New York, 1912 and 1940
The 1912 edition can go for up to $150—other prices $13-$15

Odyssey by Homer
New Pocket Classics Macmillan Company 1905 and 1930
Goes for $5 on up.

History of the Middle Ages
Dury—Henry Holt and Company, 1891
One Copy listed for $29

Pickwick Papers by Charles Dickens
Dodd Mead and Company, 1944
The 1947 copies go for $9.95--$30

Christmas Books by Dickens
Dodd Mead and Company
Nothing listed for Christmas Books
But for Christmas Tales--$19.95--$300
($300 is for the 1934 edition—No date on mine)

Mademoiselle Lavaliere
Edward Murphy
Doubleday, 1948 and 1949
Only $5.50 for good 1st edition

Six Little Princesses by Mrs. E. Prentiss
$125 if it was in great condition, others went for $26.49

Fifty Famous Fairy Tales
Whitman, 1961
$5--$22

Little Woman by Louisa May Alcott
Doubleday, 1950

Trixie Belden and the Red Trailer Mystery
Julie Campbell
Whitman 1950 and 1970
$6--$16.95

Donna Parker Books:
Takes A Giant Step, 1964
On Her Own, 1957 and 1958
Mystery at Arawak, 1962
Special Agent, 1957
Cherrydale, 1962
Goes to Hollywood, 1961
$2--$37.50

The Bobbsey Twins in the Country
By Laura Lee Hope
1950 and 1953 Goes for $8.50

The Bobbsey Twins
By Laura Lee Hope, 1950

Bobbsey Twins On A Houseboat
Laura Lee Hope 1915
Listing for 1935 copy, it went for $9.50 — $20

Heidi by Johanna Spyri
Whitman, 1954

Mystery in the Pirate Oak
Helen Fuller Orton
Scholastic paperback, 1949
Went for $1--$18.50

Miss Pickerall Goes to Mars
Ellen MacGregor
Paperback 1965
Goes for around $10

Shadow Castle
Marian Cockrall, 1945 — 1972
Paperback goes for $18.99

No Children, No Pets
Marion Holland
Knopf, New York, 1956 1st edition
Goes for $15--$56

Who Walks By Moonlight
Valentine Edition Paperback $3.75

Books that Jim Gilkison Sent To Me

Ben Hur $7.00
Harper Collins 1908

Goethe
Argyle Press: Arlington Edition 1853?

Complete Works of Horace $4.00
Modern Library 1936

Faust by Goethe $35
Hartsdale House NY
Translator: Bayard Taylor
Illustrator: Henry Clark

The Complete Works of Rabelais
Five Books of Gargantua and Pantagrul
Modern Library 1936

Practical Exercises in English $10-$12
Huber Gray Bueler
1895 Harper and Brothers

The American Looks at the World $5-$15
Carlos Baker   1944-45
Princeton University and Harcourt Brace

Reading For Writing $12.50
Studies in Substance and Form 1947
John T. Fredrick and Leo L. Ward

Writer's Guide and Index to English $5-$10

Porter G. Perrin, Colgate University
Scott, Foresman and Co. 1942

Living Biographies of Great Poets $6-$12
Blue Ribbon Books 1941 and 1946
Garden City Publishing Company

The Gambler $4-$85
Katherine Cecil Thurston
Grosset and Dunlap 1905

The Gobbler of Nimes
Mimlay Taylor
A.C. McClurg 1900

Alexander Pope: Selected Works
Edited, with and Introduction by
Louis Kronenberg
Modern Library 1948-1951

The Philosophy of Schopenhauer
Edited by Irwin Edman
The Modern Library 1928

The Philosophy of Spinoza
Editor Joseph Ratner
The Modern Library 1927

The Stories of Guy De Maupassant
Editor Saxe Commins
The Modern Library 1945

Selected Poetry and Prose of Coleridge
Donald A. Stauffer
Modern Library 1951

Irish Fairy and Folk Tales
Edited by Yeats
The Modern Library

Selected Poetry of Robert Browning
Edited by Kenneth L. Knickerbocker
Modern Library College Editions 1951

Moby Dick
Herman Melville
Edited by Leon Howard
Modern Library College Editions

Tom Jones
Henry Fielding
Edited by George Sherburn 1950

Plays by Henrik Ibsen
Introduction by Eric Bently
Modern Library College Editions 1950

Crime and Punishment
Fyodor Dostoyevsky
Introduction by Ernest J. Simmons
Modern Library College Editions 1950

Alone
Richard E. Byrd
G.P. Putnam's Sons 1938

The Black Arrow/The Misadventures.../The Body Snatchers
Robert Lewis Stevenson
Scribner's and Sons

The Merrymen/Jekyll and Hyde
Robert Lewis Stevenson
Scribner's and Sons

The Wrecker
Robert Lewis Stevenson
Scribner's and Sons

Prince Otto/Island Night's/Father Damien
Robert Lewis Stevenson
Scribner's and Sons

The Dynamiter/The Story of A Life
Robert Louis Stevenson
Scribner and Sons 1921

New Arabian Nights
Robert Louis Stevenson
Scribner and Sons 1921

The Confessions of Jean Jacques Rousseau
Modern Library New York

Twenty Years After: Volume 1
Alexander Dumas
J. H. Sears and Company New York
Edited by Lucas Lexow

The Essays of Montaigne: Volume 1
Edited by E. J. Trechmann
Oxford University Press

The Rifle Rangers
Captain Mayne Reid
S.C. Andrews 1899

English Literature
William J. Long
Ginn and Company 1919
Thackery's Works Vol 3
Clark, Given and Hooper

Wisdom of the Sands
Antoine De Saint Exupery
Harcourt, Brace and Company 1950

A German Reader for Beginners
Paul R. Pope
Henry Holt and Company 1927

Reading Poems: An Introduction to Critical Study
Wright Thomas and Stuart Gerry Brown
Oxford University Press 1941

The Old Man and The Sea
Ernest Hemmingway
Charles Scribner and Sons 1952

Shakespeare's Julius Caesar
Edited by Ashley H. Thorndike
Henry Holt and Company 1911

The Prairie
J. Fennimore Cooper
Hurd and Houghton 1871/1886

T.S. Elliot
Selected Essays
Harcourt, Brace and Company 1950

Tennyson's Poems   1887?
Belford, Clarke and Company

A Treasury of Russian Life and Humor
John Cournos   1943
Coward McCann, Inc and Company

Anastasia's Books
August 2004

The Monster at the End of this Book by Stone and Smolin

Funny Kids Songs by Kid Connection

Winnie the Pooh: Sing Along by Disney

Thomas the Train Camera Tour

Goldie Locks and the Three Bears—And Other Tales by Braken Books

Country Angel Christmas by de Paola

The Three Wise Men by de Paola

The Story of the Jumping Mouse by Steptoe (A Native American Legend)

Pocahontas Activity Book by Disney

My Friend the Teach by Leslie Eckard

My Sister the Traitor
Candice F Ransom

Waiting for Anya
Michael Morpurgo

Izzy Willy Nilly
Cynthia Voiget

Bad Girls
Cynthia Voiget

Summer of my German Solider
Bette Greene

Then Again, Maybe I Won't
Judy Blume

Blubber
Judy Blume

What Kids Wish They Could Tell You
Judy Blume

Anastasia Krumpnick
Louis Lowery

Isabelle the Itch
Constance C Greene

Charlotte's Web
E.B. White

Stuart Little
E.B. White

Dreadful Acts
Philip Ardagh

Sadako and the Thousand Paper Cranes
Eleanor Coerr

Georgie
Malachy Doyle

Born Too Short
Dan Elish

Cheating Lessons
Nan Willard Cappo

Jennifer Scales: Ancient
Mary Jane Davidson

Henry Huggins
Beverly Clearly

Henry & the Paper Route
Beverly Clearly

Ramona the Pest
Beverly Clearly

Ramona Quimby, Age 8
Beverly Clearly

Strider
Beverly Clearly

Julie of the Wolves
Jean Craighead George

Hound of the Baskervilles
Sir Arthur Conan Doyle

Adventures of Sherlock
Sir Arthur Conan Doyle

Revolting Rhymes
Ronald Dahl

Shrek the Novel
Ellen Weiss

From the Mixed up Files of Mrs. Basil Frankweiler
E.L. Kroingburg

Junie B Jones and the Stupid Smelly Bus
Barbara Park

Junie B Jones First Grader Cheater Pants
Barbara Park

Happy Birthday Samantha
Valerie Tripp (Am Girls)

Meet Felicity
Valerie Tripp

Felicity's Surprise
Valerie Tripp

Meet Kaya
Janet Shaw

Sing down the Moon
Scott O'Dell

Artemis Fowl
Eoin Colfer

Grimm's Fairy Tales
Editor Nora Kramer

The Door in the Wall
Marguerite De Angeli

What Child is this?
Caroline B Cooney

Redwall
Brian Jacques

Holes
Louis Sachar

Ferngully
Dianne Young

Dinosaurs before Dark
Mary Pope Osborne

Buffalos before Breakfast
Mary Pope Osborne

Slappy's Nightmare
Goosebumps

Welcome to Deadhouse
Goosebumps

My Harriest Adventure
Goosebumps

Hatchet
Gary Paulson

Brian's Return
Gary Paulson

The Outsiders
S.E. Hinton

Forever
Judy Blume

Give Me Back My Pony
Pony Pals

Define Normal
Julie Anne Peters

Third Grade is Terrible
Barbara Baker

Nothing's Fair in 5th
Barthe Declements

Sideways Stories from Wayside School Louis Sachar	Paddington at Work Michael Bond
So You Want To Be A Wizard Dianne Duane	A Bear Called Paddington Michael Bond
The Effects of Gamma Ray on the Man in the Moon Marigolds: By Paul Zindel	Paddington Takes to Air Michael Bond

Anastasia
New Books 2014

Maximum Ride Books by James Patterson

HIVE by Mark Walden

Maximum Ride	HIVE
Angel Experiment	Overload Protocol
Schools Out Forever	Escape Velocity
Final Warning	Dreadnought
Saving the World	Rogue
Fang	Zero Hour
Angel	Aftershocks
Nevermore	Deadlock

The Magic Tree House Series

#1 Dinosaurs at Dark
#2 The Knight at Dawn
#3 Mummies in the Morning
#4 Pirates Past Noon
#5 Night of the Ninjas
 # 6 Afternoon on the Amazon
#8 Midnight on the Moon
#9 Dolphins at Daybreak
#10 Ghost Town at Sundown
#11 Lions at Lunchtime
#12 Polar Bears Past Bedtime
#17 Tonight on the Titanic *(Library)*
18 Buffalos before Breakfast
#22 Revolutionary War on Wednesday
#23 Twister on Tuesday
#27 Thanksgiving Thursday
#29 Christmas at Camelot *(Library)*
#30 Haunted Castle on All Hallows Eve *(Library)*
#31 Summer of the Sea Serpent
#34 Season of the Sandstorm
#37 Dragon of the Red Dawn *(Library)*
#38 Monday with a Mad Genius *(Library)*
#41 Moonlight and the Magic Flute
#44 Ghost Tale For Christmas Time *(Library)*
#45 Crazy Day For Cobras (*Library*)
#48 A Perfect Time For Pandas (*Library*)

Diary of a Wimpy Kid Series by Jeff Kinley

#1 Diary of a Wimpy Kid
#2 Rodrick Rules
#3 The Last Straw
#4 Dog Days
#7 The Third Wheel
#8 Hard Luck
#9 The Long Haul

The Secrets of Droon

#1 The Hidden Staircase
#1 The Magic Escapes (Super Edition)
#7 Into the Land of the Lost

#9 The Tower of the Elf King
#33 Flight of the Blue Serpent

Star Wars: Jedi Apprentice

The Evil Experiment
The Threat Within

Harry Potter

Sorcerer's Stone
Chamber of Secret
Prisoner of Azkaban
Goblet of Fire
Order of the Phoenix
Half Blood Prince
Deathly Hallows